POLICY vs. PAPER CLIPS

*selling the corporate model
to your nonprofit board*

EUGENE H. FRAM WITH **VICKI BROWN**

Families International, Inc.
Milwaukee, Wisconsin

Copyright 1995
Families International, Inc.
Publishing in association with Family Service America
11700 West Lake Park Drive
Milwaukee, Wisconsin 53224

Library of Congress Cataloging-in-Publication Data

Fram, Eugene H.
    Policy vs. paper clips : selling the corporate model to your
nonprofit board / Eugene H. Fram with Vicki Brown. — Rev. and
Expanded 2nd ed.
        p.   cm.
    "Published in association with Family Service America . . .
Milwaukee" — T.p. verso.
    ISBN 0-87304-279-4
    1.   Nonprofit organizations—Management.   I. Brown, Vicki.
II. Title.
HD62.6.F73   1995
658' .048—dc20   95–32310

CONTENTS

THE AUTHOR'S MAILBOX   v

FOREWORD   viii

PREFACE   xi

ACKNOWLEDGMENTS   xv

INTRODUCTION   xvi

1. THE CORPORATE MODEL   1
   A Board Alternative

2. THE CORPORATE MODEL   15
   Professionalism, Flexibility, Efficiency

3. HOW THE MODEL IS STRUCTURED   31
   Intentional Simplicity

4. ASSESSMENT AND THE MODEL   45
   The CEO Cannot Be Insecure

5. THE MODEL AND THE FUTURE   65
   The Planning and Resource Committee

6. THE MODEL AT WORK   79
The Executive Committee and Its Responsibilities

7. THE MODEL CREATES A NEW CULTURE   101
Trust Is the Critical Factor

8. THE MODEL AND COMMITMENT   121
Board Members Must Be Involved

9. THE CORPORATE MODEL   135
Two Years Later

10. THE MODEL IN ACTION   143
Real Life Experiences

11. THE MODEL VS. TRADITION   153
An Overview of the Differences

12. IS YOUR ORGANIZATION READY   159
FOR THE CORPORATE MODEL?

ABOUT THE AUTHORS   176

THE AUTHOR'S MAILBOX

R ECENTLY A thank-you letter arrived in my office. A
thank-you letter is always nice, but this one was
special. It underscored in very tangible ways what a significant difference the Corporate Model can make for a
nonprofit organization, even when the nonprofit is very
successful.

The letter was written by Mary Glick, president and
CEO of a Delaware not-for-profit group with an annual
operating budget of $1 million, a paid staff of 14, and
hundreds of volunteers.

Though this nonprofit distributes more than three million pounds of food annually to needy people, her letter
wasn't about the group's work, but about how the nonprofit worked. She described developments that had
occurred in the years since she had been hired as the first
paid executive of a seven-year-old food bank. A portion
of her letter follows.

Dear Dr. Fram,

*. . . For the first several years the board and I worked on the
difficult task of moving from board management to staff man-*

agement of operations. After four years, times seemed good, on the surface. We appeared to have made the adjustment. Programs were growing, and we had just completed our first capital campaign, purchased land, and built a warehouse. Board members were enthusiastic.

I, on the other hand, was becoming concerned that, more and more, the issues I thought were "policy implementation" the board felt were "policy making" and vice versa.

Even though we didn't have any significant misunderstandings, board meetings became very stressful because I felt that it was only a matter of time before a major problem would arise. Performance reviews were even more stressful because the criteria for success kept changing. Sometimes the criteria measured something tangible but not necessarily pertinent.

Fortunately, there was a high level of trust and respect between board members and myself. Top officers were willing to take my concerns seriously and were open and supportive of my search for solutions. Luckily, during that search I received a copy of your book Policy vs. Paper Clips.

The most important aspect of your model for our board was your suggested organizational structure. We had already spent some time discussing board governance responsibilities. We had agreed that strategic planning and assessment, using meaningful, predetermined measures, were key. But until we read your book (and it is now a standard part of our board's annual orientation), we couldn't picture what kind of structure would adequately support those objectives.

Dr. Fram, your model simplified my life tremendously. Since we adopted it, I'm no longer expected to "read board members' minds" on important issues. We agree in advance on our goals, measures, and expectations. We then prioritize them and put them in writing. It is now clear to everyone involved that my job is to accomplish those goals, making the best use of volunteer and staff resources. Now our board meetings are to the point, productive, and generally last one to one-and-one-half hours.

With the growing number of nonprofits adopting your model, you may have new information you can share. I want you to know that if you plan to update your book, I'll be among the first to read it.

Best of luck and thank you.

MARY E. GLICK
President and CEO
Food Bank of Delaware

My response to Mary Glick, and to all who want to know more about the Corporate Model, is contained in this book, the second edition of *Policy vs. Paper Clips.*

FOREWORD

Peter Goldberg

S INCE PUBLICATION of the first edition of *Policy vs. Paper Clips* in 1988, a lot has happened to motivate non-profit organizations in the United States to take a close look at how they govern themselves.

The most dramatic event, of course, was the scandal at United Way of America, which led to charges of conspiracy and fraud against three top executives. Although United Way's board wasn't accused of wrongdoing, nonprofit directors everywhere asked themselves what went wrong, and many nonprofit organizations closely scrutinized and reviewed governance issues.

An even more compelling motivation for self-examination, however, has been the increasingly complex and challenging environment in which nonprofits operate. Today, more than ever before, it takes considerable time and energy to lead a nonprofit organization and to ensure that it is prepared to meet tomorrow's demand for services. For many volunteers, it is also more important than ever that their volunteer time be as productive as possible. In a world in which people live time-com-

Peter Goldberg is President and CEO of Family Service America, Milwaukee, Wisconsin.

pressed lives, time for volunteer commitments is a precious commodity.

No organization can afford to squander the hours its volunteer directors donate. At the same time, volunteer directors and executives should not be so busy "doing" that they fail to assess how they conduct business.

That's why this book is valuable for every nonprofit organization that wants to know where it is—and where it's going. Reading this book will prompt many people involved in the nonprofit sector to reexamine and redefine the roles of their board of directors, chief executive, and staff. Whether or not your organization ultimately adopts the Corporate Model, it will gain from such scrutiny. The end result of taking time for a thorough self-examination will be an organization that does its job better.

My personal experience with using the Corporate Model in a nonprofit organization is fairly recent, but already I have seen how effectively and efficiently it facilitates strategic planning by building a partnership between board and staff.

When Family Service America published the first edition of this book, 35 of our member agencies were using the Corporate Model of governance. Today, that number has increased dramatically and now includes approximately 100 of our nearly 300 agencies. Many people in our organization now understand how effectively and efficiently the Corporate Model defines roles. It provides management with the opportunity to focus on continuing concerns and policymakers to focus on the future.

Over the years, member agencies have come to appreciate many of the other strengths of the Model. Cost effective ranks high. The Model also promotes professional growth among staff by encouraging staff members to rely on their own expertise rather than on a lengthy committee process to solve problems. Staff members are what they should be—professionals who provide information and make recommendations to the board. Moreover, the board determines its strategy based on consideration of important issues rather than on fragmented committee concerns. Volunteer directors and executives accomplish more, in less time.

Much of the interest in the Corporate Model within my own organization is due to Eugene Fram, who has conducted numerous seminars and workshops for our member agencies and for countless other nonprofit groups. His experience with the Model dates to 1975.

Family Service America is publishing this second edition of Dr. Fram's book because we see it as an opportunity to help nonprofits redefine and refine roles. This edition provides additional new information while retaining crucial information from the original version.

I urge you to read this book. It is useful for anyone interested in promoting effectiveness, efficiency, and strategic planning as integral components in the management of a nonprofit organization. For organizations currently using the Model, it serves as a guidebook for continuing evaluation. Ultimately, those who will benefit most are the people you work so hard to serve.

PREFACE

E STIMATES INDICATE that more than one million non-profit organizations currently operate in the United States. Measuring their impact on society is probably impossible, although I suspect that their impact is much bigger than most Americans realize.

Consider that, in New York City alone, estimates indicate that $1 billion, or nearly five percent of the city's budget, is spent on contracted services, under which nonprofit groups provide such services as health care, job training, and youth programs.

Although most people think of the Big Apple as a center for financial services and the apparel trade, they'd probably be surprised to learn that New York City's nonprofit groups employ hundreds of thousands more people than either of these industries.

Without a doubt, nonprofit organizations—including human service agencies, trade associations, educational institutions, and professional associations—play an absolutely vital role in this country. Yet they could do their jobs even better. They could, that is, if they were better managed and governed.

As management consultant Peter Drucker has pointed out, with the exception of a small group of trailblazing leaders, management standards at nonprofits are often low.

In the book *Inside the Boardroom*, William G. Bowen, president of the Andrew W. Mellon Foundation, offers many reasons for a lackluster performance by board directors. He is quoted in a press report as concluding that some trustees see volunteer service on a nonprofit board as a vacation from the bottom line while others are seeking to "shed the 'barbarian' image that may otherwise afflict them" and therefore fail to say no to expensive, overly optimistic, or even poorly conceived proposals. Others think they know less about the work of the nonprofit, so their own expertise is less valuable. In some cases, showing an organization's financial weaknesses may mean they are under more pressure to raise funds.

In other words, the need to raise standards has never been greater. A new set of rules currently governs the environment in which nonprofit groups operate. Budgets are tight. Funding cutbacks are not only common but also increasingly painful. Along with substantial financial constraints, nonprofit organizations face increased demand for their services. In other words, resources are tighter and client and member needs are growing. Times have changed.

New management environments and directions, for example, Total Quality Management, affect all groups. Many institutions, including business, political, social, governmental, and academic bodies, have had to adjust to changing conditions.

Nonprofits cannot continue to operate as they have in the past. For most, it is no longer possible for a volunteer group of directors to be involved in the day-to-day operations of the organization. The valued executive director of the past, who had worked his or her way up through the ranks, needs more than direct-service experience in the field today. He or she needs administrative ability and a strong desire to manage an organization. He or she must be a leader, an innovator, and a communicator, all at once.

The role of the volunteer board of directors must also change. The need for change does not negate the successes achieved by volunteer boards in the past; it is merely a reflection of the fact that growth brings new responsibilities.

In addition, good governance simply makes fiscal sense. Good governance helps eliminate the many latent costs associated with pursuing activities that have nothing to do with the organization's purpose. For example, board directors who pursue projects that are worthwhile but unrelated to their mission contribute to their organization's latent costs. So does the staff human resource director who must spend an inordinate amount of time providing routine operating information to board members.

Board agendas must be cleared of operational issues, issues that paid professional staff can best resolve. Board discussions should center on policy issues—vision, mission, values, and evaluation of programs and goals.

Separating operational and policy issues is more complicated than it sounds. It requires a fundamental change in a nonprofit's culture and promotes new relationships and communication styles from the top to the bottom rung of the organization.

This book proposes to strengthen nonprofit boards and to improve their productivity through an organizational format called the Corporate Model. Although the switch to the Corporate Model is not easy to achieve, it is, I assure you, worth the effort.

The Corporate Model has been in existence since about 1975. I was instrumental in its establishment. It has been copied and used by others; those who have adopted the Model report that it works. It is most effective for the nonprofit organization that has an annual budget in excess of $500,000 and a staff of about 15 or more.

Though tried, the Corporate Model for nonprofit boards is still considered new and controversial. It flies against tradition. It has to be tailored to the needs of your organization.

This is a serious book about a serious subject, but it is far from dull reading. It is written in a lively and interesting way to capture the attention of both volunteer directors and nonprofit managers.

Read it and you will no longer have to whisper about how your organization needs to change the way it operates. You will know how to push for change. In the process, you will help make your nonprofit group a more dynamic organization.

EUGENE H. FRAM
Rochester, New York

ACKNOWLEDGMENTS

MANY people assisted us in writing and producing this book. We are especially indebted to:

James Reed, Former President, Family Service of Rochester

James Miller, Former President, Family Service Association of Indianapolis

Peter Goldberg and his staff at Family Service America, Inc., and Families International, Inc.—Ralph Burant, Janice T. Paine, and Robert Nordstrom

Most helpful was Elinore M. Fram, a volunteer director, who gave us the idea for the original book and critically read (and reread) every page of both editions.

Eugene Fram
Vicki Brown

INTRODUCTION

T HIS BOOK *is based on an exchange of letters, memoranda, and other pertinent information between two old friends who have ties to very different nonprofit organizations.*

Russ was recently appointed to serve on a traditionally structured nonprofit board. He is extremely frustrated by the board's involvement in operational issues and the plodding way in which decisions are reached. He vents his frustrations to his friend Jack.

Jack's board and line administrative experience in nonprofit groups is extensive. He is now the president and CEO of a nonprofit organization that has operated under the Corporate Model for approximately four years.

Russ and Jack are fictional characters, but the material contained in their letters and other communications is drawn from numerous case studies, records, speeches, interviews, and observations of nonprofit groups. The book draws heavily upon the author's experience as a volunteer director. Every situation or example was developed from a real nonprofit world experience. Only names and nonprofit settings were changed.

Taken as a whole, the letters and other information illustrate how a nonprofit organization can adopt the Corporate Model format for its own board. Jack and Russ provide rational solutions to the very real problems faced by nonprofit organizations across the country.

1

THE CORPORATE MODEL

A Board Alternative

9/15

Dear Jack,

I've wasted ANOTHER evening on the Yorkville board of directors! I can't begin to tell you how frustrated I am. We just give too much time to minor items such as vehicle repair bills, office dividers, and garbage contracts. The important things never seem to be discussed.

I don't have much experience with nonprofit boards, but after only one year on this one I'm ready to quit. That's pretty sad. I thought I'd be involved in significant discussions and help chart the organization's future. How incredibly naive!

Seems to me a lot of the other directors like the way the board operates. The place could be bankrupt and no one would notice.

As an old friend and veteran executive director, please give me your reaction. Is there another alternative? Or should I resign now?

Russ

P.S. I'm not sorry you recommended me for this board. I'm just sorry the board isn't more effective.

9/20

Dear Russ,

Your letter struck some nerves! Your frustration is understandable. But DON'T RESIGN! And don't be deterred from making your feelings known just because you've been on the board for only a year. You probably have some board colleagues who feel the way you do. If you're this frustrated, others must be, too. I suspect they'd make comments that echo your own.

I can relate to what's happening on your board. I grew up professionally with the system you describe. Agendas that seem endless, committee meetings that last hours, heated exchanges about personnel decisions, lengthy discussions about $100 items—but never enough time to discuss long-range needs or ways to meet them.

I'll wager that in the year you've been on the Yorkville board, you've been approached by disgruntled staff members; dealt with countless questions about individual salaries, evaluations, and promotions; and heard committee report after committee report. Very likely your board always has plans to talk about directions, priorities, and goals but never quite gets to them.

Boards like yours have been around for years. My own agency's board was structured just like it when I came here as executive director six years ago.

But no longer. We've been operating under a new board and management structure for four years now. It's called the Corporate Model. The Model takes its name from the business world because, like well-structured corporate boards, it clearly separates operational from policy issues.

Everyone who has tried the Model reports that it works. The Model makes nonprofits more professional, more flexible, and more efficient. Most important, we're able to focus more on the client groups we serve. Making the switch is well worth the end result. However, the changeover does not occur without problems.

Why? Because the Model requires a fundamental change in behavior. Directors must be willing to give up the operating power they have in traditionally structured not-for-profit groups. The top executive must be comfortable making decisions and taking risks. We're in a new era and must operate in a different kind of environment. Nonprofits are under tremendous pressure from donors, government, clients, and others who provide funds or receive services.

The Corporate Model can be adopted by nonprofit groups that have grown beyond the point where a volunteer board can oversee day-to-day activities.

It's an excellent alternative for your Yorkville board.

Drop me a note if you want more details.

I don't want to tell you more about the Corporate Model than you might want to know.

Jack

10/6

Dear Jack,

I thought about your letter and I've decided to give the job another year. But I'm not sure I'm ready to push for a whole new approach on our board—though, I must admit, your Corporate Model sounds interesting.

Have had some time to reassess. I keep telling myself that I need to readjust some people's thinking, not revise the Yorkville board's structure. After all, the board has had the same structure for many years, and the organization has done a reasonably credible job. Most of the staff are quite dedicated. Many remind me of you when you were working directly with clients.

It's definitely time for some changes. I'm staying on next year in the hope I can be a part of these changes. I think I can do it without a whole new approach.

Thanks for your support. I value your comments.

Russ

10/14

Dear Jack,

Throw my last letter away! I'm angry again and frustrated over the Yorkville board's ineffectiveness!

Why the fast turnaround? Let me tell you about last night's board "meeting."

The agenda listed a brief business session, then a discussion of long-range financial needs and ways to raise funds. With rising costs and a growing elderly population, we face some major financial hurdles. What we decide now is going to have an impact on the organization for years to come.

The executive director's report on operations was supposed to last only 30 minutes. Instead, the report opened up a tedious debate that lasted two-and-a-half hours. Happens every time any minor adjustment of fees comes up.

After that we ended up discussing whether the director should be authorized to buy a van or a station wagon to replace an aging vehicle.

By 10:45 P.M. everyone was exhausted. Long-range planning was tabled AGAIN. When Bob, a board veteran, made a parting comment, it was suddenly crystal clear to me that Yorkville can't afford to operate according to the status quo. Some big problems are emerging.

"Too bad about tabling the planning agenda," Bob said, "but I think it was a healthy airing of everyone's feelings about our fees."

I didn't tell him what I was thinking. "Feelings are fine, but we didn't accomplish anything."

We made some minor adjustments in the fee structure. None of us knows how these adjustments will affect the organization's budget. It's a critical issue. We may have to make some staff reductions if certain funding trends continue. Does this happen with your board?

And the van. We agreed with the executive director that we should buy a small van. Does such a minor decision really require 25 people and 45 minutes of discussion on your board? That's 19 person hours!

Tell me more about the Corporate Model. We need help!

Russ

P.S. The whole family is looking forward to our annual get-together at Thanksgiving. I know Paul, who's a senior now, wants to ask Jack Jr., your college freshman, what it's really like out there.

10/26

Dear Russ,

Four years ago my board of directors switched my title from "executive director" to "president and CEO."

The new title was the beginning of sweeping changes—changes that would affect everyone in the organization to some extent. I'm glad to say that my job and those of my management staff haven't been the same since. The Model made it all possible.

I don't want to inundate you with endless details about the Model. I think you'll really see its value if I can show you how it comes alive. The best approach, I think, is to send you a series of letters. Send me your thoughts, questions, and reactions as we go.

First off, let me tell you why my nonprofit adopted the Corporate Model. When I joined my organization six years ago, I was ready to manage. Board members assured me they didn't want to be involved in daily decision making. I was hired, they said, because of both my managerial and my direct-service expertise.

But problems surfaced rather quickly. The culprit—the cause of my problems—was tradition.

Some board members were used to discussing individual salaries, being involved with promotion decisions, and working directly with clients without staff involvement! Managerial responsibility was compromised. The board was seen as the final authority in many operational matters.

Even in an area as vital as the development of our budget, it was difficult to pinpoint where my responsibility and the board's began and ended. It was a system of so-called "shared responsibility," which could lead to "shared blame" when something went wrong.

Because the line of final decision making between management and the board had never been clear (on paper, the organizational chart looked like a spaghetti factory with lines going everywhere), communications were often confusing. It was not uncommon for a staff member to make an "end run" to a board member whenever he or she did not like a management decision. In one instance, I passed over a staff person for a promotion, and he called one of the most influential board members to complain. The board member (a professional with no managerial experience) told me and the staff person that I had made a mistake. I diplomatically blew my stack on that one!

I had not properly assessed how heavy a burden tradition can be. I became increasingly discouraged and wondered whether I had made a mistake in relocating and accepting the job. There was a lot of soul searching. I knew my family wasn't interested in relocating again.

Russ, I need to stop for the moment. I came in to work early so I could get off a letter to you, but now it's 8 A.M., the phone's ringing, and my administrative aide just dropped a stack of "immediate action" papers on my desk. Another letter will follow early next week.

Jack

11/1

Dear Russ,

My last letter took me to the point where I was considering quitting my job. I'm glad I didn't. Instead I took my deep concerns to the board.

I told the board I found our meetings exhausting. Our agendas were loaded with operational items, and policy issues were often postponed or even ignored. Because of the way we operated, we had countless committee meetings, overlapping concerns, and repeated questions. In turn, these drained staff time and the organization's resources. Our style meant board members were needlessly involved in operational matters. As a result, my management responsibilities were made more difficult. Worst of all, I told them, I did not think we were planning properly for the organization's future.

I was somewhat surprised to learn that about half the board shared, to some extent, my concerns about our board operation and structure. The other half felt that everything had worked for years, so why change? That first frank discussion led to the formation of a board study committee. Fortunately, it was chaired by a person with board experience in both the profit and nonprofit sectors. She really understood the need to separate operational decisions from policy issues.

Our search led us to the Corporate Model. The concept behind the Model is simply stated. The board sets policy. The top professional manager oversees operations. Eventually, this concept becomes a part of the organization's culture.

Do you think the Corporate Model sounds appropriate for Yorkville? I think I can provide the most important information. Are you interested in taking a leading role at Yorkville?

I'll wait to hear from you.

Jack

P.S. One of the reasons the Corporate Model appeals to me is that I believe a nonprofit's effectiveness and efficiency have become critically important.

- Public funding cuts (and fundraising challenges) are here to stay. Our clients have more needs than our supporters can afford, so we must focus, more than ever, on results.
- Long-term planning is key to improving results.
- Board members must set the tone for long-range planning. They need to have time to do that job well. When you consider the hectic schedules most board people have today, it's essential to conserve their time for the truly important issues.

But, Russ, the Corporate Model is not a quick fix. Change is difficult.

P.P.S. By the way, the person on your board who appreciated "the healthy airing of everyone's feelings about fees" is probably a process person. Be aware of this type of personality. It's very common to find them on non-profit boards. More about overemphasizing process and the proponents of process later.

Also, you asked me two questions I haven't yet answered. Under the Corporate Model, the board never worries about buying a van versus a station wagon. Such decisions are the responsibility of the top manager. Also, under the Model, the board approves the budget and management sets the sliding fee scale to responsibly meet budgeted income requirements. It's easy to see why this occurs if you think about the concept behind the Corporate Model.

THE BOARD SETS POLICY. THE TOP MANAGER IS RESPONSIBLE FOR OPERATIONS.

It's already 1:30 so we'll postpone the rest of the agenda till next meeting.

2

THE CORPORATE MODEL

Professionalism

Flexibility

Efficiency

11/10

Dear Jack,

I've shared your letters with several of my fellow Yorkville board members. Got some interesting reactions. The most consistent reaction was "Let's investigate." Seems I'm NOT the only one who's frustrated with the way the board operates. All three people with whom I talked want to consider a new course.

So, what do we do first?

Russ

Dear Russ,

The first step in investigating change is to get a board committee appointed to take a look at where your board is *right now*. The committee should review the present board structure, determine the need for change, and list options for the future.

Part of the work will involve a priority listing of current board problems. You've hinted that Yorkville may have to face staffing cutbacks. Other issues that jump out at me as I quickly review your letters:

- rising costs,
- an aging population,
- board members' frustration,
- lack of time for planning, which may be jeopardizing the organization's future,
- and problems in communication among staff, management, and board.

Before your board can go anywhere, it has to be convinced that the present system needs modification. If your board is typical, it will break down into several groups on this issue: people who want change, people opposed to change (some staunchly so), and what I call process people. Process people like to sit back and take a look at things. They always ask, "Have we consulted everybody?" or say, "Let's make sure we have considered everything." Often they are the people who call for a postponement of the vote, even after a lengthy discussion.

The first and third groups will be very willing to appoint a committee. Process people, in fact, like to look at options.

But remember, you want a working committee, one that's not too large. You're not looking for a 100-page report. Russ, I hope you will be a member of this committee. The Corporate Model should be an option to be examined by committee members.

I'll give you chapter and verse on how the Model works, starting next week when you come for Thanksgiving.

Jack

P.S. Process people are well-intentioned, sincere individuals. However, you have to be careful that these people don't continue to look at one angle after another until they lose sight of the committee's main job. They can keep action in limbo indefinitely!

P.P.S. It's fortunate you have colleagues on the board who are ready to take action. In my experience, boards often lose some of their best volunteers, who get frustrated and quietly resign. Their usual reason for resigning is "the pressure of current job obligations." To me, that's a covert message that the board is getting mired in minutiae. I have a good friend, an excellent volunteer director on a couple of boards here in town, who recently used "heavy job obligations" as his reason for resigning from a board. The real reason, he confided to me, was the executive director used board meeting time inappropriately, including asking the full board to review detailed scripts for slide shows.

11/16

Dear Russ,

One more quick note before I see you for the holiday.

Enclosed is the formal statement of board responsibilities developed by my board when we adopted the Corporate Model. After you read it, I'm sure you'll have questions we can discuss in person. If your board opts for the Corporate Model, one of the first things it will need is a board statement. It's the initial tool needed to achieve the separation of policy and operations required by the Model.

Jack

BOARD OF DIRECTORS' FUNCTIONS*

The board of directors establishes and monitors corporate policy. The board operates through the president/chief executive officer (CEO). The CEO, in turn, executes policy and is responsible for the prudent and creative operations of the organization. In this role, the CEO exercises leadership resulting in the effective and efficient use of board and non–board members' time. The board:

A. *Directs management*
   1. Establishes long-term organizational objectives
   2. Sets overall policy affecting strategies designed to achieve objectives
   3. Employs the CEO
B. *Judges management action*
   1. Evaluates short-term and long-term performance of management
   2. Determines whether policies are being carried out and goals achieved
C. *Approves management action*
   1. Critically reviews, approves, or disapproves proposals in policy areas (for example, major capital needs or expenditures and major contracts)
   2. Provides formal recognition and acceptance of executive decisions when related to operational concerns

*Adapted from John A. Grobey, "Making the Board of Directors More Effective,"
California Management Review 16 (Spring 1974): 25–34.

D. *Advises management*
   Acts in an advisory or consultative capacity
   on operations when sought by management

E. *Receives information from management*
   Regularly receives reports on the organization's
   performance, program development, external
   factors, issues, and so forth

F. *Acts as a public- and community-relations
   resource to management*
   Keeps the organization attuned to the external
   environment in which it operates

MEMO

Reminder: Bring this list on trip.

DATE: *11/22*
FOR: *Jack*
FROM: *Russ*
SUBJECT: *Questions to ask regarding the Corporate Model*

1. *How does the Corporate Model make a nonprofit more professional?*
2. *More flexible?*
3. *More efficient?*
4. *What are its limitations?*
5. *If the top executive has all the operational control, what kind of assessment is he or she subject to?*
6. *Who sets salaries—for example, of a top V.P.?*
7. *How do you avoid "end runs" (such as the nurse who came to me last week complaining she was being treated unfairly)?*
8. *What is the importance of the title change, say, from manager to president and CEO?*
9. *Looks to me like the Model calls for a tremendous amount of trust between CEO and board. Aren't you creating a whole new environment here?*
10. *Isn't this kind of formal and businesslike for a nonprofit organization?*

12/15

Dear Jack,

It always seems to take a while to settle in after a wonderful vacation. Thanks to you and Ann for all the good company and wonderful food. As always, our kids thoroughly enjoyed being with your two teenagers.

My primary reason for writing, however, is to thank you for all the time spent talking about the inner workings of the Corporate Model. I want to recap our talks here. Noting the most important points will make it easier to talk to others about the Model. I also want to be absolutely certain that I, too, understand it, before I ask the board to appoint a committee to evaluate our current structure.

NOTES ON THE CORPORATE MODEL

1. *The issue of increased board professionalism.* The quality of board activity improves as discussions take on a policy flavor. Important decisions can be more fully developed in meetings. The talents of board members can be used more effectively. Another key factor is that the CEO can be more creative, exploring new options and spending time on opportunities and productivity, rather than "process." The executive (CEO) can respond to board concerns in a more professional manner.

2. *The issue of flexibility.* Reducing the board's involvement with operational issues means decisions can be made more quickly and efficiently. (Under the traditional system, 35 days or longer can easily pass while a minor issue is considered by a board committee, the full board, and then implemented by management.)

3. *The issue of efficiency.* One very important benefit of the Model is that it helps reduce costs. No matter how conscientious the board member, he or she needs some staff support to make decisions. Staff support is often costly because the nonprofit uses funds to bring volunteers up to date on operational issues well understood by its professional staff.

4. *What are the Model's limitations?* Maintaining board members' commitment is the largest issue. Personal gratification is more immediate for board members when they are working with operational rather than policy questions. Board members require ongoing attention from the CEO to heighten their motivation. They must see clear evidence that their efforts make a difference and that their time is being used wisely and (for board members who are professional and business people) economically.

5. *Assessment of CEO.* Assessment should be rigorous and conducted annually. Proper assessment is critical to the successful operation of the Corporate Model. The assessment process is especially crucial for nonprofits

because the profit factor as a measurement of performance is absent.

6. *Setting salaries of executive staff.* The board sets only
the administrator's salary. The administrator sets all
other staff salaries.

7. *Avoiding end runs.* Make it clear that all personnel
issues are the responsibility of top professional management. If problems exist, they should surface in the assessment of the CEO.

8. *Importance of titles.* The titles "CEO" and "president"
signal clearly to the public who has the final authority in
all operational matters and can speak for the organization. They are not ambiguous. The terms "manager" or
"executive director" do not carry the same clout.
Managers and executive directors (because of the history
of nonprofits) are often viewed as "hired hands," not as
professionals with final operational authority.

9. *The amount of trust required under the Corporate Model.*
The Model creates an entirely new working environment. It calls for a working relationship based on trust
and mutual respect. All communications go through the
CEO. He or she is the person accountable to the board
and is the representative of the staff. This is why the
assessment of the CEO must be thorough and why it is
so critical to the success of the Corporate Model. This

working environment is a new kind of "culture." Jack stressed over and over that it is THE key ingredient in the Corporate Model.

10. *Formality.* Yes, it is more formal. But this is a natural outcome of any growing organization, whether it be for-profit or nonprofit.

Anything else you think I should add, Jack? Will look forward to hearing from you.

Russ

12/20

Dear Russ,

Got your recap yesterday. It's excellent. Will be interested to hear from you after you share it with some of your fellow board members.

By the way, I was talking to a friend of mine yesterday. He's an executive director of a nonprofit group with an annual budget of $5 million. He estimates that his organization spends at least $50,000 a year in staff time to serve his board's various committees.

I suggested to him that the Corporate Model could cut these costs, because it eliminates or sharply reduces board involvement in operational matters.

Jack

P.S. Russ, I hope I haven't made the process of switching to the Model sound too easy. You'll want to be certain your fellow directors at Yorkville realize that they will face the following problems:

- Making the switch is a touchy process.
- Tradition will probably hamper you all the way.
- Despite the fact the Corporate Model has been around for years, the concept is still considered very new.
- If you adopt it, you'll probably be among the first nonprofits in the area to do so.
- Some board members will be afraid of losing control.

- Some staff may fear that your organization will become "too businesslike."

Finally, your executive director has to be ready for the significant increase in responsibility. If an executive director is incapable of or unwilling to change, nothing can be done until the nonprofit gets a new exec. However, Russ, I am well acquainted with Yorkville's executive director, Joyce Thomas. I have a lot of confidence in her ability.

I'm absolutely convinced that the Corporate Model makes it possible for a board to concentrate on the major policy issues before it. In turn, that means the organization is better able to serve its clients.

THE BOTTOM LINE IS: THE ADVANTAGES OF THE CORPORATE MODEL FAR OUTWEIGH THE DIFFICULTIES IN MAKING THE SWITCH.

DIRECTOR

C.E.O.

End runs belong on the field, not in the office.

3

HOW THE MODEL
IS STRUCTURED

Intentional Simplicity

Dear Russ,

Last night I took a few minutes to review our correspondence and realized that in the flurry that always seems to accompany the end of the year, I'd forgotten to send you a copy of my agency's organizational chart.

Some of your board colleagues will probably be surprised at how uncluttered it is. The simplicity is intentional. As you'll note, our structure provides for only three standing committees—Executive, Planning and Resource, and Assessment.

The Executive Committee is composed of myself, our corporate officers, and an at-large member elected by the board. The committee acts for the board between meetings, subject to later board ratification; sets the monthly agenda; reviews reports for board discussion; and appoints members to all standing and *ad hoc* committees.

The Executive Committee, which usually meets monthly, is our most active committee. You can expect the same would be true for Yorkville or any other locally based nonprofit. Some people become concerned about giving the Executive Committee too much power. In practice, however, committee members consult with others on particularly difficult decisions or if the committee is so evenly divided that the decision could go either way. I've yet to see a situation in which the Executive Committee has operated in an imprudent manner.

The Planning and Resource Committee assists the CEO in long-range planning. (The CEO directs the long-range planning effort and is the person chiefly responsible for developing the vision of what the organization might become in the future.)

The Planning and Resource Committee also monitors the activities of the *ad hoc* committees. All of our *ad hoc* committees are established for a specific purpose and then disbanded when their work is complete. For example, our nominating committee operates only when needed to fill board vacancies and to develop a slate of new officers.

The Assessment Committee, with the CEO, develops the organizational goals, subject to review by the Executive Committee and ratification by the full board. Most of the goals are yearly ones; others cover a two- or three-year span. After the goals are established, this committee is responsible for an objective assessment of the CEO and organizational performance. This is based on goal attainment as well as on detailed review of the fiscal audit completed by our CPA firm.

Recommendations of the Assessment Committee are used as part of the base for establishing goals for the following year and for the CEO's performance and salary evaluation.

Special note: Instead of having financial operations monitored by the Assessment Committee, some organizations choose to establish a separate Finance Committee. The decision to have such a committee should be based on two factors: the level of financial support needed by the CEO and the complexity of the organization's finances. If a Finance Committee is established, it will take responsibility for assessing the organization's financial health and for bringing financial issues into sharper focus.

Specifically, the Finance Committee would:
- Work with the vice president of finance to review financial statements.
- Set policy on endowment investments, subject to board ratification.
- Meet annually or semiannually with external auditors.
- Have direct access to internal auditors.
- Review the formal management letter.
- Review operations of financial policy.

In our case, we find three standing committees sufficient. Our Assessment Committee is able to handle these duties along with the rest of the performance assessment. Your board, if it adopts the Corporate Model, may want to add a Finance Committee or in some other way vary this organization chart. Let me know what questions people there have after reviewing this information.

Jack

P.S. A note of caution—if you go too far beyond the three standing committees, you run the risk of having what I call the "spaghetti factory" organizational chart.

THE STRUCTURE OF THE CORPORATE MODEL BOARD

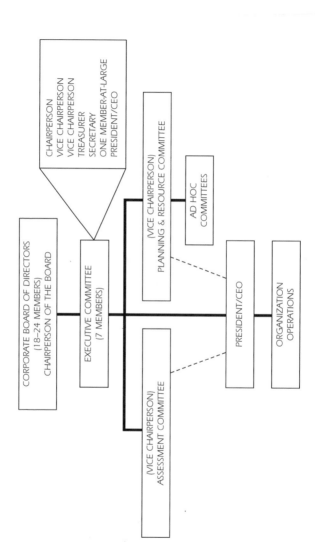

CORPORATE BOARD OF DIRECTORS
(18–24 MEMBERS)
CHAIRPERSON OF THE BOARD

CHAIRPERSON
VICE CHAIRPERSON
VICE CHAIRPERSON
TREASURER
SECRETARY
ONE MEMBER-AT-LARGE
PRESIDENT/CEO

EXECUTIVE COMMITTEE
(7 MEMBERS)

(VICE CHAIRPERSON)
PLANNING & RESOURCE COMMITTEE

AD HOC
COMMITTEES

(VICE CHAIRPERSON)
ASSESSMENT COMMITTEE

PRESIDENT/CEO

ORGANIZATION
OPERATIONS

1/12

Dear Jack,

I passed your organizational chart and note around and asked for reaction. Nearly everyone had the same four questions.

1. Why a board of 18 to 24 members? (Our board has 30 members now.)

2. If we had to reduce the size of our board, how would we do it? (We want both expertise and experience on our board.)

3. How do you get by without a standing building committee? Personnel committee?

4. Are you, as president/CEO, a voting member of the board?

The people I've talked to on the Yorkville board are impressed with how efficient the Corporate Model appears on paper. Your organizational chart certainly reduces the layers of board governance and focuses on board responsibilities.

At the same time, we don't want a committee structure so streamlined that it creates an elite group of board members (those who really know what's going on) and leaves the rest of the board to merely rubber stamp decisions. We want to be sure we would not sacrifice board teamwork just for the sake of simplicity.

Russ

Dear Russ,

We've been hit with a tremendous snowstorm. Can't get anywhere this morning. Gives me an unexpected opportunity to answer your letter and relax at home with an extra cup of coffee.

Before tackling your questions, I'd like to comment on a phrase in your letter. You said that your Yorkville colleagues were impressed with how the organizational chart I sent you "reduces the layers of board governance."

What the Corporate Model really does is eliminate some board activity that is better handled by management. I'm not nitpicking here. I want to make an important point and, at the same time, pave the way for answering your questions.

The Corporate Model is based on the premise that good management is not the same as good board governance. A second key concept is that you can't have one without the other. In other words, to improve the leadership and effectiveness of management you must make board governance more effective.

The organizational plan I sent was adopted here with these concepts in mind. Keeping them in mind, let me go on to answer your questions.

1. If you look at the number of board members on other nonprofit boards, you'll find that 18 to 24 members is an unusually small number. The crucial thing is not how big

the board is, but whether it works. Ours does. It's a workable group because the number is manageable. Also, remember that under the Corporate Model your board wouldn't be staffing a lot of committees that discuss issues already reviewed by staff.

2. From our experience here, I recommend that if you adopt the Model, you pare down the size of your board. You can do that gradually. As terms end, do not refill them. You'll find some people will leave voluntarily. Be prepared, however, for one or two directors who are opposed to the Model to leave with some ill feelings.

Board members who are particularly interested in hands-on involvement may opt to serve in a different volunteer capacity within the organization. You don't have to sacrifice expertise or experience, but the makeup of the board will inevitably change. That's O.K. It's even healthy.

3. We get by without a standing personnel committee (or building committee or others you could name) by appointing *ad hoc* committees as needed. We don't, for example, need a standing personnel committee, because everyday personnel issues (hiring, firing, and promotions) are the responsibility of management. However, if we want to determine whether to change our pension plan (a major policy issue), we appoint a board committee to work with staff to investigate the alternatives. When its work is completed, the committee is disbanded.

4. As president/CEO, I am a voting member of our board. Our board took this route for symbolic purposes—to put the top manager who represents the staff on the same level as the volunteer board. You might tell your colleagues that I've never cast the deciding vote in the four years we've worked under the Model. Nor have I heard of another CEO being put in this position. The power to vote makes you a peer, not a powerhouse.

Jack

P.S. Some states may not permit a nonprofit's president/CEO to be a voting member. You'll need to check requirements in your state.

P.P.S. We don't have an elite group of board members who run the show. What we do have is an active board. Every member does work that is valuable to the organization and meetings are held for specific purposes. Most of my board members have what I call time-compressed life-styles. They appreciate limiting their board activities to what's important and specific.

P.P.P.S. Reducing the number of board members is not as unusual as you may think. Many nonprofits with boards of 75, 100, 125 or more persons (which is not uncommon for national associations) have found large boards to be expensive and unwieldy. Such boards also tend to consolidate power in the hands of a few committee people.

Reminds me of a story I read in the paper recently about a national association that was planning to trim its board from 75 members to 21. I remember the executive director's exact quote: "It's very difficult to have a discussion with 75 people."

By the way, it FINALLY stopped snowing.

1/21

Dear Jack,

What a night! Thought I'd dash off a quick note despite the hour (11:30 P.M.) and tell you to keep your letters coming.

Tonight, at my suggestion, the Yorkville board voted to appoint a committee to review our present structure and determine whether we need to make some changes. I've been appointed, along with five other board members, to investigate options for the future.

In my recent letters I've been so interested in getting information about the Model that I've neglected to tell you about the growing frustration of the board. Tonight, after a particularly long discussion on minor issues, I couldn't restrain myself any longer.

I pointed out that because we're so mired in operational issues we haven't tackled major policy or long-range planning issues for more than six months. Believe me, that comment opened up some lively discussion! It was obvious the time had come for this board to take a look at its future.

Our first committee meeting is next week. I'm ready for it. I want this committee to seriously consider the Corporate Model.

Be prepared. I know there will be questions. I appreciate your continuing interest.

Russ

1/25

Dear Russ,

I'm ready for your questions. Fire away as they come.

By now you realize just how completely I support the Corporate Model. I look forward to helping you determine whether it is THE answer for Yorkville.

First, though, some quick thoughts:

Be aware that some board members and staff will look at the Model as "an insensitive business approach." You'll probably find these people (particularly staff) fearful that management will become cold, distant, and unfeeling. My contention is that you can have a big heart and still have good management.

Don't underestimate the concern about board members' involvement. True, handling policy and strategy issues simply isn't as "hands on" and immediately rewarding as handling operational issues. However, there are ways to make sure board members' involvement is truly meaningful and satisfying. Down the road I'll give you more pointers in this area.

For now, good luck with that first committee meeting. I hope the rest of the committee is as committed as you are to finding a better way for your nonprofit group.

Jack

P.S. If you review our correspondence, you'll see we've come a long way in a short time. We've discussed the need for changing nonprofit board structures as well as the efficiency and effectiveness underlying the Corporate Model. We've also covered a synopsis of the Model's working structure.

YOU'VE GOT THE OUTLINE. FROM THIS POINT ON, WE NEED TO ELABORATE ON THE PARTS OF THE MODEL. THE PARTS ARE CRITICAL, PARTICULARLY THE OPERATION AND PRODUCTIVITY OF THE ASSESSMENT COMMITTEE.

ASSESSMENT AND THE MODEL

The CEO

Cannot Be Insecure

Dear Jack,

The six of us who were appointed to take a look at the structure of the Yorkville board met for the first time tonight. It was a productive session, with each committee member agreeing to take on a specific assignment.

As you might have guessed, I'm in charge of bringing in as much information as possible on the Corporate Model. We had time for only a brief discussion, but once again I find that you're right on target. Initial questions are focused on the whole issue of assessment.

Any thoughts, guidance, or direction you can give me in this area will be useful.

Russ

1/31

Dear Russ,

Seven months ago I was one of several speakers at a large national meeting. I spoke at length on the structure and inner workings of the Corporate Model. Two people who followed me on the platform made some pretty interesting comments about "living with the Model."

The first one, Fred Jackson, is the top executive of a human service agency in New York State. The other, Sarah Tobin, is the head of a nonprofit trade association in the Midwest.

Luckily, a friend of mine taped most of that session and I have almost all of their comments. I'm enclosing excerpts from Fred's speech, roughly transcribed by my administrative aide.

I've temporarily misplaced Sarah's comments but will forward them when I find them. I hope to do that sometime within the next week. The information should be pertinent to your investigation.

Jack

Russ—
Fred Jackson's comments.
His NY nonprofit has had
the Model for 8 years.   Jack

Living with the Model

A lot of people aren't quite comfortable with the whole concept of assessment. It scares them, I think, because they don't really understand what it means or how it works. Let me illustrate my point with a story.

Less than a month ago, the chairman of my board of directors and I were in Detroit, giving a workshop on the Corporate Model to executives and board members. Eight of the 20 persons present were executives from various nonprofit agencies, ranging from a developmental center to an automotive trade association. They happened to be sitting near each other in the center of the room, which made it easy for me to see all of their faces when I began sharing the assessment report completed a few weeks earlier by my board. Included in the report was the board's evaluation of my performance.

Twenty minutes into my presentation it was obvious that all eight of the executives were totally surprised— you might say aghast—at my candor.

"Fred, do you really want this information, including some criticisms of your own performance, to get out?" I was asked.

"Certainly," I said, "it's already public knowledge."

"Are you also comfortable knowing your board members are out inquiring about your performance—asking how Fred Jackson is doing?"

"Not only am I comfortable with it, but I also expect it," I answered. "The people doing the talking are members of my board's Assessment Committee doing their job. They need to talk to others to determine how we're performing."

Looking around the room I noticed that the other 12 persons in the room—mostly board members from various other Detroit nonprofit organizations—were also surprised by my comments.

"The president/CEO of a nonprofit organization cannot be an insecure person," I said. "If I live in fear that I'll lose my job, I won't accomplish anything."

I told that group, and repeat here today, that I believe the most important job of the board of a nonprofit is to find the best possible person to manage the organization, then stand back and let that person manage.

In turn, the most important job of the top staff person in any nonprofit is to manage to the very best of his or her ability—then stand back and allow one's management performance to be thoroughly evaluated.

The assessment process does not mean that Fred Jackson, president and CEO, has to have an adversarial relationship with his board. The directors of a nonprofit organization and the head of that organization are on the same team. However, like virtually any other kind of team, its members have different roles and responsibilities.

At the beginning of every year, directors on the Assessment Committee and the nonprofit's top staff person agree on joint goals for the organization. These goals, which must be ratified by the entire board, should be achievable but challenging. Because of the nature of nonprofits, some goals can be measured only in highly qualitative terms. By that I mean that you can measure achievement only by sampling information through personal comments. To the extent possible, however, the goals set should be ones you can quantify.

On my own board, assessment is very thorough and takes place annually. That doesn't mean it's done all at one time. Assessment occurs throughout the year, depending on how Assessment Committee members decide to divide their tasks. After completing its entire investigation, the Assessment Committee makes its report to our board. It doesn't have to be done this way. I know of some Corporate Model boards where assessment updates are given periodically throughout the year.

The CEO has to understand that the full board must make some subjective judgments based on the Assessment Committee's findings. The CEO must be strong enough to live with these judgments, because under the Corporate Model, the CEO is told what the board wants but not how to achieve it.

I might add here that the CEO must also be strong enough to handle criticism. The CEO is going to be criticized—that happens in every creative, dynamic organization. What upsets some managers is that the criticism is made public in a written report.

You might ask, "Who would want such a job?" After eight years with the Model, I can honestly say, "I like working this way!"

As the president and CEO under the Model, I can be far more creative than the typical manager of a traditional nonprofit organization. My responsibility is to live within the mission, budget, and guidelines set by the board. My board doesn't get involved with how many computer disks, notebooks, or paper clips I buy. I don't have to go to the board for each contract negotiated during the year. I don't get locked into endless discussion about personnel issues.

We're an organization on the move.

Assessment is a report card. It tells me, the board, and the community how well the organization is doing what it set out to do.

2/1

Dear Russ,

I got lucky. Here's the rough transcript of Sarah Tobin's speech.

Jack

Russ—
Sarah Tobin heads a non-
profit trade association
in Missouri.

Life Under the Corporate Model

I was a true skeptic. As far as I was concerned, the Corporate Model was nothing more than an ego trip for the executive. When I was asked by my board to consider it, I remember thinking, "How can restructuring and new titles help? If we need to fix something, just tell me what it is and I'll work harder for a few more hours and take care of it."

At the urging of my board, I reluctantly agreed to accept the Model.

Three years have passed since then, and one-time skeptic Sarah Tobin can now stand before you and tell you that the Model has indeed changed the very nature of our organization. Take, for instance, my own position.

It is probably easier for the board to fire me. Heretofore, when so many operational matters were shared decisions, the outcome was also a shared responsibility. If something went wrong, I shared the blame. Now, if something goes wrong, it takes no guesswork to figure out who is responsible. There is little opportunity to pass the buck or to plead that I was only following directions.

Within the first few weeks after my board made the switch, I realized that if I weren't mature enough to accept that level of responsibility and accountability, I probably did not deserve my job. I told myself, "If I can't stand that much heat, I'd better get out of the kitchen."

Actually, the Model has reduced the "heat" I feel, which never was oppressive. Now I have more flexibility, more freedom to act, and waste less time and motion. I'm not providing a group of decision makers with enough information so that they can come to the same conclusion I had reached.

In Total Quality Management terms, I've been empowered to do my job. What my board wants from me are results that can be reasonably measured by means of quantitative or qualitative methods. No question—qualitative information is open to broad interpretation. That's where I must rely on those making the assessment to understand they are reasonable individuals making reasonable (not perfect) judgments.

Participatory management between board and staff may help everyone feel busy and involved, but unfortunately it may involve people in the wrong things and fail to use their talents in the most effective way. I think more carefully now about my decisions, but knowing that they are mine and that I am trusted with the authority to make them is a blessing. I have discovered that these new arrangements are invigorating and do not bring about more "heat."

Dear Jack,

The excerpts from the two speeches gave me real insight into the role of the CEO, the critical importance of assessment, and the value of assessment for the organization. What I need now is some basic information about how to set up an Assessment Committee.

Russ

Dear Russ,

Typically, seven to nine persons make up the Assessment Committee. Members are appointed by the board's Executive Committee. (The president/CEO is not a voting member of the Assessment Committee but attends most sessions.) The individuals appointed must be willing to confront hard issues and make recommendations. They must be conscientious and thorough.

The first order of business is to work with the CEO to establish personal and program goals for the organization. These are developed from a list compiled by the president/CEO and the Assessment Committee chairperson.

Next, the committee maps out its work and agenda over a period of time. At Yorkville, for example, your committee might decide to assess an established "wellness program" every two years but choose to evaluate a new staff-development program at the end of each of the next three years. Obviously, fiscal goals are monitored each month and evaluated closely every year.

The committee chairperson assigns individual tasks for the year. This work can be done easily if it is divided fairly among members. Usually, individual tasks take each person a total of one or two days a year, plus a few meetings with the entire committee.

Each person on the committee takes the steps necessary to get the data he or she needs (for example, through internal data or interviews with staff, interviews in the community, or surveys). Each person then prepares a four- to eight-page written report. A typical program or project assessment report will include the following:

- a brief history,
- a summary of goals and objectives,
- a list of staff, organization, and facilities,
- budget (including funding source and trends),
- assessment of strengths, areas in need of improvement, continuing appropriateness, and
- recommendations.

The full committee does not need numerous meetings throughout the year. The committee chairperson's job is to make sure things get done as scheduled. The chairperson also coordinates the various written reports and sends periodic updates on the committee's work to the full board.

At least once a year, the entire Assessment Committee meets with the organization's outside auditors. Part of the meeting is held without management present—one of the few times that management is excluded from any meeting. Management understands that this procedure does not reflect on the integrity of the management group. In fact, when the Assessment Committee is initially established, this process should be presented as standard procedure. Typical questions asked during this meeting are:

- Have you noticed any unusual transactions or large payments?
- Was management cooperative during the audit?
- Is there anything else you want to tell us in the absence of management?

In the business world, these questions are asked by board audit committees. Many large accounting firms provide complimentary booklets describing how audit committees operate. You might want to refer to one of these booklets to determine the procedure for your Assessment Committee.

At the end of the year, the full committee reviews all committee reports and financial reports. It then summarizes these reports and submits its final document to the full board. This final report includes an assessment of the president/CEO based on the overall findings of the committee.

Do you have other questions about assessment?

Jack

P.S. I hear your high school senior has applied to my son's college. Do you think Paul will go there?

2/13

Dear Jack,

I do have one more question. What if the Assessment Committee doesn't do its work well?

Seems to me that if that happened, your system of checks and balances fails. The organization could end up being run more for the staff than for the people it is supposed to benefit. Management could run wild in setting salaries or fees or fail to deliver a quality product.

I'm sure you remember the big scandal at the United Way of America's national office a few years ago. Seems to me there were serious issues involving people at the highest levels in the organization.

And what about the more recent scandal involving the Foundation for New Era Philanthropy, which turned out to be nothing more than a modern-day pyramid scheme?

Right?

Russ

P.S. Paul is waiting anxiously for college acceptance letters. His first choice is your son's school.

2/16

Dear Russ,

I was waiting for you to ask me about the scandal at United Way in connection with the issue of proper assessment. Virtually everyone involved with nonprofits remembers this scandal because the top executive's salary was so generous and the perks so extensive. In fact, charges of fraud and conspiracy were filed against top United Way managers.

In my opinion, the United Way and New Era Foundation scandals are dramatic examples of what potentially can happen if management has no checks and balances. Management, as you so aptly put it, can run wild. Remember though, the potential for self-serving behavior exists whether a nonprofit is traditionally structured or operates under the Model.

For that matter, the same thing can happen in profit-making organizations. I suspect that you've seen news articles about companies whose managers establish highly lucrative retirement plans for themselves—"golden parachutes"—in case their firms are purchased by or merged with another organization. A nonprofit's management team under the Corporate Model is not likely to run wild, however, for the following reasons.

From day one, any nonprofit organization that adopts the Corporate Model also has to be committed to the idea of rigorous assessment, conducted annually. The board must determine whether there are any problems with the

Assessment Committee and move as quickly as possible to correct them.

It has been my observation, and the observation of others, that the Model helps nonprofits build a cadre of superior managers.

Many nonprofits are evaluated by outside accrediting or review organizations, which also ascertain whether the nonprofit is benefiting client groups. This information helps to supplement a reasonable, although not perfect, system of checks and balances provided through the work of the Assessment Committee.

Jack

P.S. I should tell you what happened at United Way in the wake of that scandal. The board addressed the situation by revising audit committee procedures and adding an outside advisory committee for the audit committee.

P.P.S. To help your committee with its work, I've included an outline showing how one organization, which has had a lot of experience with the Model, handles its assessment process. Use it as a guide (my own organization found it very helpful) and feel free to adapt it to meet your own board's needs. For example, the outline shows how the initial negotiations on goals can be handled by the chair of the Assessment Committee or the board chairperson. In your case, you may want the board chair to take on this assignment.

THE ASSESSMENT PROCESS

How Evaluation Is Accomplished

- **Joint Goal Setting**
  - Begins with CEO, using past year as base
  - CEO negotiates upcoming year's goals with board chairperson or Assessment Committee chair
  - CEO and Chairperson or Assessment Chair complete revisions
  - Executive Committee reviews goals
  - Executive Committee sets time frame (1–3 years for individual goals)

- **Assessment Committee Evaluation Process**
  - Committee determines appropriate times for evaluation
  - Assessment chairperson coordinates
  - Committee members interview/analyze data, etc. (time commitment for this task: 6–8 hours a year for each committee member)
  - Each person writes section of assessment report
  - Chairperson compiles report
  - Committee reviews full draft
  - Committee sends report to Executive Committee for comment
  - Assessment Committee meets with external auditors
  - Executive Committee sends report to the full board

- **The Assessment Committee Report**
  Can be as long as 50 or even 100 pages,
  with each section containing
  –Brief history
  –Summary of goals and objectives
  –Staff, organization, and facilities
  –Budget (funding sources and trends)
  –Strengths
  –Needed improvements
  –Continuing concerns
  –Recommendations

Basic Principles of Evaluation

- Rigorous assessment of the CEO and the organization are necessary to ensure the organization's future
- The assessment process clearly establishes executive authority and responsibility
- All nonprofit groups need to allow for management flexibility and creativity
- The management team requires latitude for risk-taking—some projects will fail
- Evaluation is designed to assess outcomes of policy implementation, not how operations took place
- The focus is on productivity and outcomes
- Evaluation can highlight the need for policy change
- Board understands no executive performs perfectly
- The assessment team must be reasonable and fair-minded

- Assessment is not adversarial in practice or spirit
- Evaluation is an on-going process

Jack

P.S. Let me add one final basic principle to this outline. That is, assessment has to be more thorough in a not-for-profit than it is in a for-profit organization. Without shareholders, profits, and customers who can make choices, measurement of results is much more difficult.

If your committee at Yorkville ultimately recommends that the Corporate Model be adopted, it must also stress the role of assessment.

PROPER ASSESSMENT IS THE KEYSTONE—THE VERY HEART— OF THE MODEL.

5

THE MODEL AND THE FUTURE

*The Planning and
Resource Committee*

2/22

Dear Jack,

Let me update you on where we stand now. My Yorkville committee is forging ahead. After the two committee sessions we held this week, no one still thinks we can salvage our current structure.

The three persons investigating the current board functions came in with a very critical report. They had interviewed Yorkville's key staff people, from Joyce Thomas on down, as well as the members of the board's Executive Committee.

Joyce was very candid, as were Executive Committee members and top staff. The message is clear. We have no firm sense of where Yorkville is headed. In particular, its long-term financial stability is a matter of real concern. Joyce wants to spend more time managing and less time reporting to the Yorkville board and its committees. The Executive Committee recognizes the need to devote more time to planning.

However, as you predicted, a few influential board veterans just don't buy the idea that the board should set policy and leave operations entirely to management. These veterans are pretty nostalgic about how things used to be when Yorkville was a small organization. As you warned me, some even fear that if they give up their role in helping run things around here, Yorkville will no longer be the caring organization it's known to be! It's obvious we're going to face a touchy situation with these directors. I may be calling you for advice if we find things getting too hot!

On my own committee, I sense a growing interest in the Corporate Model as an alternative. And that brings me to my next request. In one of our conversations at Thanksgiving, you mentioned that the work of the Planning and Resource Committee is every bit as important as that of the Assessment Committee. What more can you tell me?

Russ

2/26

Dear Russ,

Simply stated, strategic and tactical planning are your lifelines. If planning is incomplete or otherwise inadequate, you may jeopardize the future of your organization.

Under the Model, the CEO is the person chiefly responsible for planning. The job of the Planning and Resource Committee is to assist the CEO in short-term and long-range planning. That may sound like a minor supportive role, but believe me, it isn't.

As you know, in the case of human service organizations, board members represent the community. With trade or professional organizations, the board represents the membership. The board has the primary responsibility for ensuring that the programs and services a non-profit organization offers are in the best interest of the clients it serves and the community or membership it represents.

Specifically, the Planning and Resource Committee provides the "radar" for the board. It also acts as its "traffic cop." It provides the radar by evaluating whether the organization is being correctly positioned to meet the future needs of clients. (The roughly equivalent function in the for-profit world would be marketing research.) As traffic cop, it helps make certain that board projects are completed and wise use is made of volunteer efforts and time.

The members of this committee, more than any other, work closely with the organization's staff. The staff provides much of the background information necessary for the committee's work. Recently, for example, my own organization considered whether our program should expand outside our traditional service area. The Planning and Resource Committee's job was to investigate.

Four committee members met with various key staff members who would be involved in any expansion effort. Committee members and staff decided together how to proceed. Staff members then completed most of the actual background work. The end product was a joint board/staff report that is now before our full board.

At the same time, a second Planning and Resource subcommittee was working with staff to determine whether we should develop 24-hour access for certain client services.

Over the course of a year, the Planning and Resource Committee is likely to complete a number of specific reports, which are then reviewed by the Executive Committee and finally by the full board. That means many people consider, discuss, and evaluate an issue before the entire board votes.

The chairperson of Planning and Resource coordinates the committee's work and updates the full board on its activities at each regular monthly board meeting.

Jack

P.S. I've got a call in to a colleague whose organization has used the Model twice as long as my organization has used it. I'll ask him to add to what I've told you. He's due back soon from a business trip. Will write again after I've talked to him.

Dear Russ,

I talked to the colleague I mentioned in my last letter, the one who is a real veteran of the Corporate Model.

He believes the Corporate Model structure has allowed his nonprofit organization to move smoothly through a period of growth. When the Model was adopted nine years ago, his nonprofit had an $800,000 budget, a staff of 30, and a total of three offices. Today, he oversees a budget of $3.5 million and a staff of 100 persons working in 12 locations.

If his board hadn't switched to the Model, he doubts the organization would be where it is today. Board emphasis on policy making and planning was needed in order for the nonprofit to grow. He gives a great deal of credit to the efforts of his various Planning and Resource Committee members over the years.

The locations of the nine newest branch offices and the dates they were opened were critically important for his nonprofit, because initial start-up costs were unusually high for the kinds of services they provide. He said his Planning and Resource board members did a tremendous job analyzing data provided by his staff. Committee members made valuable suggestions.

The decisions made by the full board have almost always followed the recommendations made in joint reports from Planning and Resource Committee members and staff. To date, my colleague says, his nonprofit has been ahead of the competition in offering services.

He also noted that Planning and Resource Committee members on his board do a major five-year long-range-planning report periodically and update it annually. Long-range-planning documents entail considerable staff time, he said, but they are well worth it in the end.

He told me more about specific projects, but I think what I've told you so far gives you an idea of how critical a role Planning and Resource Committee members play.

It goes almost without saying, I think, that the interaction between staff and board committee members contributes significantly to the creativity within an organization.

Jack

3/5

Dear Jack,

I appreciate how the Corporate Model gives an organization the structure it needs to grow and how it contributes to creativity at all levels.

But I still have a few very basic questions:

1. Can you give me some guidelines on setting up a Planning and Resource Committee?
2. How often would such a committee meet?
3. Is the CEO involved in all meetings?
4. How involved should the staff be?

Russ

3/10

Dear Russ,   .

Let me take your questions in order.

1. How you set up the Planning and Resource Committee really depends on your organization's needs at a particular time. Are you emphasizing financial planning, long-range planning, or short-term planning?

We have eight to ten members on our committee, but there is no perfect number. The key is flexibility. This committee should be set up according to what is necessary at a given time.

2. As I've indicated before, our entire Assessment Committee typically meets as a full group no more than four times a year. The full Planning and Resource Committee may meet more or less often, depending on the issues under consideration.

Subcommittees, also known as *ad hoc* committees, meet as needed. They deal with a range of topics, such as personnel policies, OSHA requirements, and long-term space needs. After making a report to the full committee, *ad hoc* committees are disbanded.

3. Generally, the CEO attends all major committee meetings. He or she may or may not serve on subcommittees, depending on the information and guidance needed by the group.

4. Staff input is critical. Professional staff make major contributions to board policy decisions through their involvement with the Planning and Resource Committee. (As CEO, I strive to foster an atmosphere in which my staff members feel free to express opinions in Planning and Resource meetings to board directors and to the administrative staff.)

When confronted with a particularly difficult issue, an excellent means of communication is a board/staff workshop. Such a workshop brings staff and members of the Planning and Resource Committee together in a relaxed setting. Such workshops contribute greatly to our efforts to plan for programs. The interaction between board and staff enhances the quality of our decision-making.

At times, the Corporate Model has been criticized for eliminating informal communication between the board and staff, since all operational communications are routed through the Executive Committee and CEO. As a practitioner and keen observer of the Model, I find this criticism unfair. Board members and staff members have ample opportunity to work together on task force projects that really have an impact on the organization. Such activity benefits the organization and isn't just social contact.

Jack

P.S. I can't emphasize enough that board members and the top executive of a nonprofit organization must work together in an organized way to analyze the risks and opportunities that affect a nonprofit.

Too many boards have been content to analyze proposals endlessly. Others, to avoid conflict, have tended to rubber stamp proposals made by vocal or overly aggressive board members. These boards have not truly participated in the challenging act of establishing policy and direction for their nonprofit group.

The times are changing. Boards are being held much more personally accountable for their actions by the community and by legal statute.

P.P.S. THE CORPORATE MODEL PROMOTES ACCOUNTABILITY. IT REQUIRES THE BOARD AND THE CEO TO WORK TOGETHER TO PAINT THE BIG PICTURE FOR THE ORGANIZATION. IT THEN HOLDS THE CEO ACCOUNTABLE FOR IMPLEMENTING THAT VISION.

THE PLANNING AND RESOURCE COMMITTEE PLAYS A MAJOR PART IN PAINTING THIS PICTURE. IT'S ROLE IS TO HELP THE ORGANIZATION AND THE CEO LOOK AHEAD TO THE FUTURE.

I like how our CEO moves! He manages all of
the day-to-day operations so we can
concentrate on looking ahead.

6

THE MODEL AT WORK

The Executive Committee
And Its Responsibilities

3/18

Dear Russ,

Have to tell you about a conversation I had Saturday night.

Ann and I were invited to a large dinner party where we were introduced to a number of guests. During the evening, one person happened to mention his involvement with a not-for-profit group in our community. Naturally, I was interested, particularly when I heard him note with some pride that he was a member of the organization's Executive Committee.

"We have a REAL BOARD," he told me. I asked him to explain what he meant, and he said that "a real board tells its executive director exactly WHAT TO DO." I made a mental note to avoid that nonprofit if I ever decide to look for a new job. Then I changed the subject. I didn't think it was appropriate to tell him what I really wanted to say: "You don't have a real board. What you have is a parent–child relationship."

When I got home that night I thought of you and the concerns of your committee. What Yorkville has now, and what many nonprofits have clung to for so long, is a parent–child relationship. Like all such relationships, they come in many different forms.

But Yorkville is discovering, albeit painfully, as are so many other nonprofits, that organizations outgrow the old structure and must find a new structure if they are to reach maturity.

You and I haven't yet talked about the work of the Executive Committee under the Corporate Model, and now seems an appropriate time to tackle the subject. I want us to approach the topic in a way that will help your committee really understand how things change under the Corporate Model.

Let me suggest a method that I think should make it clear. The next time your restructuring committee meets, ask your colleagues to come up with a list of four or five issues that theoretically could come before the Executive Committee of a not-for-profit group.

I'll then take those same issues and point out two different ways of responding to them. One will apply to Executive Committees with the traditional structure, wherein the board assumes a parental role. The other will apply to Executive Committees with the Corporate Model.

Jack

3/27

Dear Jack,

Somehow you always seem to anticipate what my committee members need to know in order to truly understand the Corporate Model.

Just before I got your last letter, I made a list of the responsibilities of the Executive Committee. My list was based on notes I took when we talked over the Thanksgiving weekend. Here's what it said.

Under the Corporate Model, the Executive Committee:
- sets board meeting agendas
- acts for the full board between meetings, subject to later ratification by the full board
- receives all reports from the Assessment and the Planning and Resource Committees
- appoints all members of standing, *ad hoc*, and advisory committees

After making the list, I asked myself, "How is this Executive Committee different from any other?" I knew I would be hard pressed to answer that question. I was about ready to drop you a note asking for your help when your letter arrived.

~~I reported your offer and everyone liked your sugges-~~ tion. After some discussion we came up with five issues we'd like you to address:

1. Development of the annual budget

I'll be home later, dear. . . . Meeting with a group of directors. I wonder what office operations they'll change this month!

2. Budget deficits and cash-flow problems
3. A personnel issue, for example, the hiring of additional minority staff
4. Employee grievances
5. Interpersonal relationship between the board chair and the CEO

The committee is eager to explore this entire area. Is it possible for you to respond before my committee meets again on April 17?

I know you're putting in a lot of time for us and I want you to know I appreciate all the effort.

Thanks,
Russ

4/2

Dear Russ,

I like your suggested topics. What I plan to do is address each issue in a separate memo. This will make it very easy to see the difference between the traditional board structure and the Corporate Model board. (I also know my schedule. If I try to do it all at once it might not ever get done!)

I'll forward each memo as soon as I can. The first one is attached.

Jack

MEMO

TO: *Yorkville Committee on Restructuring*
FROM: *Jack*
DATE: *April 2*
SUBJECT: *The Executive Committee and the Annual Budget*

THE SCENARIO: The organization is developing its annual budget.

THE TRADITIONAL BOARD

The Executive Committee oversees the entire budget process. Although it may delegate significant responsibility to board finance committee members and to individual staff members, particularly the top staff person, it remains in charge of the overall budget process. (I have seen situations in which the Executive Committee views budget development as a responsibility it shares with the top paid executive. I have also observed situations in which the board's finance committee gets involved with deciding line items and budget details.)

By the time the budget is submitted to the full board for approval, the Executive Committee will probably have had countless budget meetings, sometimes lasting hours. Operational issues (such as individual salaries, maintenance schedules, and equipment purchases) may have been covered at length. In some organizations, the finance committee chairperson, not the executive director, presents the budget to the board.

The day the budget is approved by the full board, most Executive Committee members feel they know every paper clip the nonprofit expects to purchase in the next 12 months!

This "top down" budget process has a long history. It dates from the time when board members of a nonprofit organization were viewed as having the expertise in fiscal and managerial issues. Professional staff, on the other hand, were perceived as experts in delivering varying types of service.

THE CORPORATE BOARD

One of the premises of the Corporate Model is that volunteers — part-timers, if you will — cannot and should not be expected to shoulder the financial and managerial burden that the budget process demands. (The considerable burdens of their own professions prevent them from acquiring the necessary knowledge relevant to the nonprofit organization.) In today's world, no reasonable business could operate effectively with such part-time expertise. A nonprofit should not be expected to operate this way either.

The Corporate Model structure recognizes that the president/CEO and the staff have the most thorough knowledge of the needs and resources of the organization. The Executive Committee expects the president/CEO to work with the staff to develop the budget within policy guidelines set by the board. It tells the president/CEO that he or she is responsible for developing a budget and for presenting it to the Executive Committee for questions and discussion. Subsequently, the budget is presented to the full board by the president/CEO.

Because the board must ultimately approve the budget, it must understand the budget process, ask tough questions, and be aware of the organization's financial needs and resources. But that does not mean the board usurps the president/CEO's responsibility to develop the budget. Instead, the board may appoint members to serve on a budget review committee (for example, the treasurer, a representative from the Assessment Committee, and a representative from the Planning and Resource Committee).

The Corporate Model recognizes that budgets are best developed from the bottom up under the direction of the CEO, the person who knows most about the organization and has responsibility for executing policy directives. The president/CEO keeps the board informed of progress and, if necessary, educates the board on the budget process. He or she submits a complete and detailed document for approval and stands ready to answer questions and respond to board recommendations.

After the budget is approved, the Corporate Model board gives it back to the president/CEO and says, in effect, "Now it's your job to live within it."

MEMO

TO: *Yorkville Committee on Restructuring*
FROM: *Jack*
DATE: *April 6*
SUBJECT: *Deficits and Cash-Flow Problems and the*
        Work of the Executive Committee

THE SCENARIO: For a variety of reasons, revenue has been much less than projected for the XYZ Nonprofit Association. If the current situation does not change, the organization will have a deficit of $18,000 for the entire year. The association also has an immediate cash-flow problem. Substantial payments due from two contracts have been delayed for three weeks. Without these payments the association will be unable to meet its payroll two weeks from today.

THE TRADITIONAL BOARD

The Executive Committee has been in session for hours. The board chairperson has delayed a trip in order to attend the special meeting. One can almost feel the tension in the room. Everyone has questions.

"Why did this happen? What do we need to do to turn the situation around? Can we charge more for certain services? Should we revise the entire fee structure? Is it time to eliminate one or more programs? If we trim staff, what will the consequences be?"

After a lengthy, detailed discussion, the committee takes two steps. It authorizes the association to borrow $15,000 to cover the next payroll.

The Executive Committee also asks the board finance committee to look at options for covering the entire expected deficit. The board chairperson is concerned about the amount of time the finance committee must spend in the next few weeks to investigate the situation and come up with a viable solution. However, she sees no alternative.

Before adjourning the meeting, the board chairperson turns to the two board members who are authorized to sign for a loan and asks if they can get together the next day. The chairperson is dismayed to learn that one of the two must be out of town on business for three days. New arrangements are made.

Finally, late into the night, the Executive Committee adjourns. Every member is well aware that meetings like this one will probably occur again.

THE CORPORATE BOARD

The Executive Committee is in session in its regularly scheduled monthly meeting. The chairperson calls the meeting to order promptly at noon.

One of the agenda items is a report from the Planning and Resource Committee. The president/CEO and the committee chairperson bring the Executive Committee up to date on the deficit situation. (Eight weeks previously, the president/CEO had informed the entire board that revenues were below pro-

jections and that a deficit was likely to occur if changes were not made. The chief problem, the president/CEO had said then, was that the association was facing new competition in one major service area. In addition, contract payments in another area were delayed. The CEO had suggested that the Planning and Resource Committee meet with him and key staff members to see what could be done.)

The Planning and Resource Committee chairperson reports that the recent review session was productive. As a result of that meeting, the president/CEO had:

- *put a four-month freeze on hiring*
- *delayed the opening of a new satellite office*
- *moved to make its key service area more physically attractive*
- *conducted additional staff in-service training to smooth out some newly identified problems that were adversely affecting cash flow*
- *taken steps to move more quickly in making planned program changes discussed four months ago by the president/CEO and members of the Planning and Resource Committee.*

The president/CEO, in his report, tells the Executive Committee that initial results from these changes are encouraging. The association should be able to avoid the projected deficit. "One thing that really helps," he says, "is that the association is able to move quickly when we see a problem ahead of us."

The president/CEO also notes that he borrowed $15,000 to cover the anticipated cash-flow problem caused by the unex-

pected delay in the contract payments. (The president has the authority to borrow up to $75,000 for short-term cash-flow problems.)

Following other reports, the chairperson adjourns the meeting. The Executive Committee session ends at 1:40 P.M., just a little later than usual.

Two weeks later, the entire situation was reported to the full board in detail for discussion, review, and ratification. However, during this two-week period several knowledgeable board members were informally apprised of the situation by the president/CEO. This avoided the surprise element no board should tolerate.

MEMO

TO: *Yorkville Committee on Restructuring*

FROM: *Jack*

DATE: *April 8*

SUBJECT: *The Executive Committee and Personnel Issues*

THE SCENARIO: The nonprofit agency ABC has been criticized for not having enough minority staff members. Because ABC—a large, well-known organization—serves primarily urban residents in a major U.S. city, board members are concerned about the criticism.

THE TRADITIONAL BOARD

The Executive Committee meets in a regular session. Spread out before each member are a half-dozen copies of articles criticizing the organization for having few minority staff members. The articles have appeared in the local newspaper in the past week.

Emotions run high at the meeting. Many board members feel the organization has been treated too harshly in the media. The hiring and training of minority staff members has been an agenda topic at least three different times in the past six months. (Actually, the topic had first been raised 18 months ago in the Personnel Committee, which had not fully considered the question because it had been tied up for months settling a grievance related to health benefits for a retiree.)

Twice previously, the Executive Committee had discussed the minority staff issue but had run out of time and tabled it for later consideration. During a third discussion, the board was unable to agree on a solution. Instead, because the Personnel Committee agenda was still full, a special ad hoc *committee had been formed. The* ad hoc *committee was due to report back in another month.*

Executive Committee members say the existence of that special committee should have been pointed out in the newspaper articles. They spend most of the remainder of the meeting discussing how to counteract the negative publicity the organization has received. Several members maintain that if the organization had a board member with public relations experience, this situation would never have occurred.

THE CORPORATE BOARD

This Executive Committee did not read about the lack of minority staff in newspaper articles. The criticism was contained in a report presented at the last meeting by the board's Assessment Committee. The report pointed out that the CEO should have taken more decisive action in this area.

At today's meeting, Executive Committee members agree that the organization must take steps to hire and train more minority staff. The president/CEO agrees that this issue needs to be a higher priority on his operational agenda. He says he will discuss the topic again in four weeks. He also will update the personnel plan developed two years earlier. Evidently that plan is not achieving its objectives.

MEMO

TO: *Yorkville Committee on Restructuring*

FROM: *Jack*

DATE: *April 11*

SUBJECT: *Employee Grievances and the Executive*
           Committee

SCENARIO A: A high-level staff member calls the board chair-person at home one night to complain that he had not been given a raise. The chairperson has worked with this staff member many times over the years and respects his work.

SCENARIO B: A member of the Executive Committee receives a call from another staff member who complains he was given a negative evaluation by his supervisor. The staff member says the evaluation was "unfair" and asks the board member to intervene on his behalf.

THE TRADITIONAL BOARD

SCENARIO A: The board chairperson calls the executive director and tells him that in order to be "fair" to a highly competent staff member, the matter should be brought to the Executive Committee. The chairperson presents the case at the next Executive Committee meeting. For 20 minutes, committee members discuss the work of the employee in question. They also question the executive director about the situation. Com-

mittee members ask him to leave the room while they consider the matter. Finally they agree to a pay increase of $200 a month. The raise is made retroactive to the previous month.

SCENARIO B: After receiving the staff member's call, the board member calls the organization's executive director and asks her for more details. After listening to her report, the board member says he agrees with the evaluation of the staff member. He tells the executive director he will report their conversation to the staff member who called.

THE CORPORATE BOARD

SCENARIO A: The board chairperson tells the high-level staff member to take his request for a raise directly to the president/CEO. The chairperson is well aware that by stepping in to solve the problem he would undermine the authority of the president/CEO.

SCENARIO B: The Executive Committee member tells the staff person to discuss the negative evaluation with his supervisor again. If they cannot agree, he should discuss the situation with the president/CEO (the supervisor's immediate boss). Later the president/CEO calls to say, "I appreciate the way you handled this matter. We were able to work out the problem in a face-to-face meeting."

MEMO

TO: *Yorkville Committee on Restructuring*

FROM: *Jack*

DATE: *April 13*

SUBJECT: *Interpersonal relationships between board chairperson and the CEO*

THE SCENARIO: Newly elected board chair is being briefed on responsibilities by outgoing board chairperson. At the moment, the outgoing chairperson is discussing his relationship with the CEO and the nonprofit's staff.

THE TRADITIONAL BOARD

"People are always telling me that they see my car parked outside the agency an awful lot. It's true that sometimes I feel as though I'm 'in residence' here. I spend a lot of time in meetings with the CEO, and though that takes a great deal of the CEO's time, I believe my hands-on approach has been very helpful for the organization. A lot of staff feel comfortable talking with me about various issues and problems. I guess you could say I've developed my own informal communication channels with staff members. Many of them view me as the authority — practically the parent — here. I've felt I've been able to contribute a lot working this way. The first thing I recommend you do when you take over this position is get yourself a regular parking space just outside the front door."

THE CORPORATE BOARD

"Our CEO is the professional in this organization. She's an excellent manager with expertise in the field and that's why we hired her for the top job. My job, as board chair, has not been to stand by her side at all times, debating her every move, and discussing problems with staff. I've viewed my role as being a supporter and board leader. That means I've appeared here as needed and made myself available as an adviser to the CEO and to others designated by her.

"At the same time, I recognized early on that I had as much of a responsibility as the CEO to build the communication channel between us. We met and talked about how best to work together. As a result, both of us have been very willing to pick up a phone and talk about key issues. We've developed great professional respect for each other and are willing to listen even when we have a difference of opinion on a subject. I have no doubt you, too, can develop this same kind of excellent working relationship.

"As chair, I've also been responsible for what I call 'institutional memory'—in other words, the history of this organization—and for keeping the board on track in terms of policy issues. It's been my job, and now will be your job, to maintain the Corporate Model and to ensure new board members are trained in how it works. I can't overemphasize how critical this training is. If it isn't undertaken on a regular basis, new board members can become confused about their roles and responsibilities.

"Being board chair carries a lot of responsibility, but that doesn't mean you have to end up practically living here."

4/15

Dear Russ,

Just a few last thoughts about the Executive Committee under the Corporate Model.

Do remember that all reports and actions from standing committees go through the Executive Committee before going to the full board. All *ad hoc* committee reports go through both the Planning and Resource and Executive Committees before they are submitted to the board. This system promotes information flow and leads to effective and efficient meetings, which, in turn, do not waste your board members' valuable time.

I hope that my scenarios help you understand why I favor giving the CEO the right to vote. It is a sign of authority. Since the CEO represents the staff, it also gives the staff a voice on the board, albeit indirectly.

The Corporate Model does allow for outside advisory committees, appointed by the Executive Committee. Advisory committee representatives can attend board meetings, except when the board goes into executive session. Outside advisory committees should work closely with a nonprofit's staff to ensure that the information they provide will improve operations.

Jack

P.S. THINK OF THE EXECUTIVE COMMITTEE AS AN EXPEDITING GROUP. BY DOING ITS WORK WELL, IT ALLOWS THE FULL BOARD

TO CONCENTRATE ON IMPORTANT POLICY ISSUES.

P.P.S. WE'VE NOW COVERED THE MODEL'S STRUCTURE AND THE ASSESSMENT, PLANNING AND RESOURCE, AND EXECUTIVE COMMITTEES—IN OTHER WORDS, ALL THE PARTS OF THE CORPORATE MODEL.

7

THE MODEL CREATES
A NEW CULTURE

Trust Is the Critical Factor

4/18

Dear Jack,

After last night's meeting my Yorkville committee is close to recommending that we adopt the Corporate Model. However, two areas of concern remain.

We think that we need to know more about the new culture created by the Corporate Model. We also need more information about how to keep board members truly involved without the ego satisfaction that often comes from dealing with operational issues.

Your assistance has been invaluable. Can you help us with these two final areas?

Russ

4/22

Dear Russ,

Your timing is terrific.

I'm going to be in Yorkville on business for two days in mid-May. I have meetings with my counterpart in Yorkville on Thursday and Friday, May 20 and 21, and will be tied up both days and Thursday evening.

If you don't mind having a houseguest Friday night, I'd be willing to meet with your committee Friday evening and Saturday morning. We could devote the first session to "culture" and the second to "involvement."

Would your committee members be willing to give up part of their weekend on such short notice?

Jack

P.S. How about dinner with you two at that great restaurant we enjoyed so much last time Ann and I were in town? I should be free by 4:30 that Friday.

4/27

Dear Jack,

We're set for your visit. Only one committee member can't make it Friday evening. Saturday morning looks clear for everyone in the restructuring group.

I'll treat you to dinner before the Friday night session. Saturday we'll start at 7:30 A.M. I promise to have coffee and bagels on hand.

Both sessions will be at my house. If the weather is good we should be able to get in at least nine holes of golf after Saturday's meeting ends!

Russ

P.S. Jack, I plan to tape record both sessions. My administrative aide will transcribe and edit the tapes, so I'll have a record of our discussions. I'll send you copies.

5/23

Dear Jack,

The edited transcript of our Friday discussion is attached. Please note:

Unless otherwise indicated, you are the person speaking. Comments and questions by other speakers are in italics.

I'll send you the edited transcript for the Saturday session soon.

Russ

First Session
"The Model Creates a New Culture"

We've been writing to each other—through Russ—for so many months I really feel that I know all of you. I've been looking forward to our get-together tonight. I really enjoy talking about the Corporate Model. Thanks for giving me a forum!

When you talk about the new kind of culture that must exist for a Corporate Model board, you're talking about something intangible but very real. Let me start off with three stories, each of which illustrates what that new culture is all about. Afterward, I'd like you to ask me any and all questions you might have on this topic.

My first story is about my friend Sam, who told me over lunch recently about his problems as a member of the board of a nonprofit organization. Sam is a busy guy who agreed to join this board because he really believes in what the organization is doing. Yet, Sam is finding the board job more time-consuming and frustrating than he ever imagined.

Sam's board has devoted a major part of the past three months to hiring a new vice president. The position has been discussed by the board's personnel committee, by the Executive Committee, and by the full board. Sam is on the personnel committee, which spent three long evenings discussing the wording in the job description.

"Everyone knows we need to fill that position soon, but the process seems to be taking forever," Sam told me. He was particularly upset that the top candidate for the job got tired of waiting and decided to withdraw his application.

Sam was amazed when I told him I'd hired a new vice president just last month and my board wasn't involved at all. I said we had selected a terrific person and made the changeover in record time. Before lunch was over, we discovered that my new V.P. was the very person who had given up on Sam's organization!

The point to remember here is that presidents/CEOs under the Corporate Model have much more responsibility for their organizations than do executive directors in traditional nonprofit groups. They can move faster and be more creative. They can hire and fire without endless committee discussions. They are responsible for all personnel changes below their level. The Model, in fact, is specifically designed to delegate a high level of authority to management. "Board culture" is extremely important because board members must be at a point where they feel comfortable with this level of delegation.

Obviously, the CEO should routinely keep the board informed about personnel changes at a high level. However, the Corporate Model board generally has little interest in changes relating to operational staffing. The one outstanding exception may be when the CEO wants to hire an "unusual staff member," that is, someone who is not filling a traditional staff position. Although the CEO still has the responsibility for hiring, he or she should review the need for the position with the board. The board should reverse the CEO's decision only if the long-term prospects for the position and the costs involved do not fall within the approved budget strategy.

By the way, for information purposes, I take a few minutes each quarter to highlight staff changes and activities for my own board.

In brief, with the Corporate Model, directors respect the CEO's ability to run the organization.

My second story concerns a nonprofit organization that operates under the Corporate Model. Recently, the president/CEO discovered, quite by accident, that a former staff member in the personnel office has copies of some confidential payroll documents.

When the CEO asked the former employee for the copies, the individual refused to give them to her. The former staff member feels that he has a right to the copies because they relate to the work he performed for the organization.

Well, the top execs of many nonprofits would run immediately to the board for help. However, this CEO recognizes that she's paid to be a problem solver. She wants the board to know about the situation but also is concerned about protecting the organization, the board, and its individual members from any legal liability that may result from the situation.

This CEO made an appointment to see a lawyer and invited the board chairperson to accompany her. With the guidance of the lawyer, the CEO verbally reported the situation to the board along with the lawyer's recommended actions.

The important thing is not how this situation was ultimately resolved, but how the chief executive handled it. On a traditional board, the problem would have been dropped like a "hot potato" into the hands of board members. On the Corporate Model board, the president/CEO plays quarterback. As I'm sure you are aware, that's a significant difference.

My third and final story is about a nonprofit organization I'm sure you'd recognize. There are countless organizations just like it throughout the country.

This particular nonprofit is large, and it operates a significant number of programs. Recently a new director was hired to run these programs. The board selected the person for the job and determined her salary with only modest attention to the advice of its executive director. Not surprisingly, the new program director does not have much respect for her boss. In fact, when she has a problem with a program she takes it directly to the board.

Unusual? It happens more often than you realize. However, it never happens on a Corporate Model board that functions as it should. In reality, you can't have a Corporate Model board unless you have a chief executive officer who is really in charge of operations.

As I've mentioned several times before, a board of directors that adopts the Model places a great deal of responsibility and authority in the hands of its president/CEO. The board must be sure that the individual it selects for the job not only can handle the position but also will be comfortable in it. Once that decision is made, board members must place their faith and trust in their new executive.

Trust is an essential ingredient here.

If board members do not trust and respect their CEO, one of two things will happen. Either the Model will fail or the CEO will leave.

It's particularly important that the board chairperson and CEO personally trust each other. The chairperson must view the CEO as a competent executive, not as an expert in direct service who needs help with management activities. Whether the CEO came up via the direct-service route is unimportant. As CEO, his or her first job is to manage. In return, the members of a Corporate Board must stand back and let him or her do the job.

Now let's open this up for questions. I suspect you have some.

Jack, how do you know when you've achieved this new kind of culture?

Think of your organization as a ship. The board of directors determines the ship's destination. The president/CEO has command of the ship and is responsible for getting it to its destination in the most efficient and effective manner. If your nonprofit—your ship—works this way, you're on course.

It used to take three board people to do what
our CEO now does easily on her own.

I like your analogy, Jack, but can you give us a couple of other real-life examples of how this new culture works? Something more "everyday" in nature than the case of the employee with the confidential documents?

I can think of two examples immediately.

As you may have guessed, I've served on a number of nonprofit boards over the years. The *volunteer president* of one of these organizations, a nonprofit association with a traditional structure, always made it a practice to notify the full-time executive director when he planned to take a vacation. In essence the volunteer president was asking, "Is this an appropriate time for me to be gone? Can you handle things while I'm away?" In some cases, the executive director even delayed making his own travel plans until the two of them had conferred.

This kind of situation wouldn't exist with the Corporate Model. It would be assumed that the CEO is in control of the organization. Out of courtesy, the chairperson might inform the CEO when he or she would be out of town.

Should the CEO decide to be out of town at the same time, he or she must arrange for appropriate staff back-up. As a courtesy, the CEO should inform the chairperson about travel plans. Let me note here, however, that only once in four years has it been necessary for my chairperson and me to be in contact while one of us was out of town.

My other everyday example of the culture at work is from my own organization. Two years ago we had a fairly new employee who wanted to see his methods of improving staff morale put to work.

This individual wrote a letter to each board member, informing them that staff morale was poor. He also detailed his suggestions for improving the situation. Because everyone received the letter, the issue was raised at the next Executive Committee session.

Two members of the committee opened the discussion by saying, "This is an issue for management, not the board." I was asked to handle the situation and to provide information about it. That kind of comment wouldn't have been made on a more traditional board. The board probably would have wanted to get in and personally investigate.

But let me add a note of caution here. Sometimes an individual with such a concern may be alerting the board to a growing, unrecognized problem. Board members walk a fine line in these situations.

Jack, I've been on the Yorkville board for a long time now. Until recently, it wasn't unusual for us to meet every couple of months without the executive director. Would that ever happen on a Corporate Model board?

No. The CEO's involvement is central to the success of the Corporate Model. Here's where that issue of trust comes into play. For the full board to meet without its top executive really says, "We can't trust you to run this place." Under normal conditions, the only time the board or any important committee should exclude the CEO is when the Assessment Committee meets with the outside auditors to review the yearly audit and management letter.

If there's a problem with the CEO, it'll be obvious in board assessment reports. If the CEO is going to be fired, he or she will know it. Termination won't come as a surprise to anyone.

Do you think an exec who has worked only under a more traditional structure can make the transition to the Model?

Absolutely—as long as that individual understands his or her new role and is comfortable in it. Let's talk specifically for a moment. I've known Joyce Thomas, your executive director, for some time now. She has excellent administrative skills. She and I have even had some conversations about the Corporate Model. I suspect she'd welcome the change.

On the other hand, I've had many executive directors tell me there's no way they would want the kind of responsibility I have. This kind of person is not a candidate for an organization with the Corporate Model.

O.K. We have an executive director who could make the switch but I wonder about a board chairperson. He is used to having an active program committee study every issue from every angle. He wants to know about every nickel the organization spends. So what happens if you have a CEO who can do the job but the board chairperson doesn't want to relinquish power?

It's simple. If your chairperson can't change his or her style, you need a new one—someone who's comfortable with new ways of doing things. For example, you won't need countless board program committee meetings—that's why you have staff.

The Model allows the CEO a measure of fiscal latitude. Just how much latitude should the CEO have?

Once the board approves the operating budget for the year, it monitors the organization's financial status monthly and annually. The CEO reports monthly expenditures and income by major areas. At each regular monthly meeting, the CEO also informs the board about any budget developments and exceptions. A thorough assessment of how the organization is doing financially is conducted annually by the Assessment Committee.

My board's trust is shown most graphically by the fact that I can borrow, on my own, up to $100,000 on a short-term basis when we have a cash-flow problem.

I can understand how fiscal latitude gives the CEO the freedom he or she needs to spend money on behalf of the organization. What I don't understand is who in the organization is responsible for fund raising? Isn't that an area in which the CEO should follow the board?

When it comes to fund raising, and this is a significant area we haven't really covered before, the board and the CEO have mutual responsibility.

As President and CEO in an organization using the Corporate Model, I'm really the advance guard when it comes to fund raising. First and foremost, I have to be alert to all the places where I can raise funds on my own. This involves everything from developing grant requests to understanding where public funds can be obtained to knowing about national and local sources that might support my organization's goals. Obviously, I don't do all this alone. My staff is there to assist me.

My next responsibility is to work closely with directors on the board who have development backgrounds, skills, contacts and who can expand the effort to attract resources from a wider range of organizations and individuals. Let me give you an example of how this works with my board.

A year ago, my staff and I identified a need in our community that we felt our organization was well equipped to meet. After we designed a program that would assist the specific population in question, I took our proposal to the board. I explained the reason for proposing the program, and board members concurred with me that we needed to move ahead. We discussed fund raising objectives outlined in the program proposal, and over the next few weeks I asked several board directors to assist me in opening doors or making calls. At times board members made calls on their own. At other times we made joint calls. We evaluated each situation to determine the best approach.

Let me sum all this up with a simple analogy. When it comes to raising funds, consider the president and CEO the forward scout looking for a potential source of funds. The board—the cavalry—is called in to support that effort and broaden the base of support. In other words, the scout gives the signal, but the cavalry is needed to take the objective.

Do you ever make use of board directors in your scouting party?

Yes, I do. If you are lucky enough to have a forward-looking board member with well-developed fund-raising skills, you'll probably quickly discover, as we have, that the individual can give you new insights into achieving your goals. For example, I have a terrific board director who helped lead us into an entirely new field of service and opened many donors' doors. All of this resulted from the experiences and information she gained on another board in another city.

Should all board members be required to be involved with fund raising?

The simple answer is No—just those who have done it before or are willing, with some coaching, to give it a try. However, you do want to maximize your board members' contacts. That may involve teaming someone who does not usually get involved in fund raising with an experienced hand if the inexperienced person knows a potential donor.

If you adopt the Corporate Model, your CEO will need to be an assertive leader when it comes to fund raising, but all of you, as board members, must play an active supporting role. Let me emphasize here that a nonprofit board does not abdicate its fund-raising responsibilities just because it hires a strong CEO.

Unless you have other questions about fund raising, I have just one further point I want to be sure to make tonight. Everyone on your board should be making an annual contribution. Certainly the amount depends on each individual director's personal situation, but even a token amount is significant. When you're developing proposals, especially grant proposals for foundations or corporations, funders want to know whether all members of a board are behind the organization.

I like the fact that the Model makes the job of the top executive more entrepreneurial. However, because the CEO has so much authority and because the board places so much trust in the individual, isn't it easy for the CEO to overstep his or her boundaries?

It happens. When it does, it's the board's job to inform the CEO that he or she has taken on too much authority. I was guilty of that myself recently. I signed a long-term contract that should have gone first to the board. I typically sign routine contracts on my own, but the longevity of this one meant it should have had board approval first, even though the dollars involved with the contract were very small. I recognized my error when it was pointed out by my board chairperson, who asked for formal board ratification of the contract. None of us does our job perfectly. But a CEO does have to recognize who is the ultimate authority. In a nonprofit organization it's the board of directors.

Doesn't the Model require more trust between board and CEO than you would find in the for-profit world?

It does. I don't believe you need as much trust in the for-profit world because the bottom line can give you a reasonably clear (not exact) indication of how the CEO is performing. In the nonprofit world you have no bottom line, except the one that says income must match expenses. Board directors must trust in the ability of the person they have selected to do the job. They must hold that person accountable for doing the job.

Jack, we have to wrap this up for tonight if we're going to get together early tomorrow. You've convinced me of just how important this new environment, this new culture, is to the Model.

It seems that trust under the Model is like trust in a marriage. You don't want to marry a person you don't trust. You also don't change to the Corporate Model unless you have, or can hire, a president/CEO in whom you can place a reasonable amount of trust.

THE MODEL AND COMMITMENT

Board Members

Must Be Involved

5/29

Dear Jack,

Here's the edited transcript from our Saturday session. I've followed the same format that I used in the transcript of the Friday-night session. Italics are used to identify other speakers.

Russ

P.S. The restructuring committee is meeting early in June to begin drafting our report to the Yorkville board. Will keep you posted on developments.

Second Session
"Board Members Must Be Involved"

Good morning! We're here to talk about "involve-ment." Let's get right into it.

I'm not at all surprised that you want me to address this topic. Whenever I talk about the Corporate Model to any group, I'm invariably asked one question: "If a board isn't involved in the day-to-day concerns of an organiza-tion and meets less frequently, won't directors soon lose interest in the organization?"

My answer is always the same. "No they won't, not if you keep them informed and they have specific, worth-while tasks to accomplish for your not-for-profit group."

People volunteer as board members of nonprofit groups for all sorts of reasons. Some have benefited, first-hand, from services provided by the nonprofit. Some have skills they want to utilize. Others volunteer because they want to expand their personal or professional con-tacts. Most care deeply about what the organization is seeking to achieve.

One could go on and on. It's the job of the chairperson and the CEO to understand why a person has volun-teered and to match that person's skills and interests to the needs of the nonprofit.

Let's talk specifically about Yorkville for a moment. We'll assume your board has adopted the Corporate Model. President/CEO Joyce Thomas and her staff hypothetically are now deciding whether to buy new

equipment, increase insurance coverage, fire the custodi-
an, hire a new program director, choose new furniture
for the reception area, revise budget forms, revamp the
accounting department, and so forth.

In the past, board members had a big part in those
activities. Now you and your fellow Yorkville directors
are free to grapple with the bigger issues. For example:

- What kind of organization is Yorkville going to be
  in the future?
- Should it provide all of the services it now provides?
- Should it provide any new services?
- What does the financial future look like?
- What's the impact of rising costs?
- Is there a need for more emphasis on fund raising?
- How would staff cutbacks affect services?

When they tackle these kinds of questions board members truly invest themselves in the organization. Let me
explain by painting a picture of what three Yorkville
directors might, theoretically, end up doing on your
Corporate Model board.

Director A is particularly interested in finding out
whether programs that have been in existence for some
time are still viable or whether they should be revamped
or discontinued. When the chairperson asks Director A if
she'll serve on the Assessment Committee, she willingly
agrees.

Director A's first assignment is to work with two other
committee members to evaluate Yorkville's client om-
budsperson program. Their task is to examine the pro-

gram and make recommendations about its future. Their findings and recommendations will be communicated to the full Assessment Committee and then to the Executive Committee and the full board.

At the same time, Director B, who has agreed to serve on the Planning and Resource Committee, volunteers for a joint board–staff *ad hoc* subcommittee assigned to evaluate the feasibility of starting a new pilot program. A community group has approached Yorkville and asked that it consider providing certain limited off-site services for the elderly.

Director B will head the five-member group charged with determining whether this kind of program is appropriate for Yorkville. The subcommittee must determine whether such a service fits within the organization's spectrum of services, whether Yorkville is capable of entering into such a venture, and whether Yorkville would be viewed by the community as an adequate service provider. The subcommittee expects to make a report to the full Planning and Resource Committee within two months.

Director C, a local accountant, is particularly interested in the financial health of the organization. He agrees to serve on the subcommittee assigned to investigate options for improving Yorkville's financial position. One of those options involves hiring a part-time development specialist for the organization. Director C anticipates his group's report will be in the hands of the full board within the next 12 weeks.

Note that all three of these directors work with fairly small groups on specific tasks. They have clear goals to achieve. When their tasks are done, all three directors will feel that their talents have been utilized in important ways to benefit Yorkville.

Members of Corporate Model boards will stay interested and involved in their nonprofit organizations if they are convinced that their activities have a purpose and serve the organization. I know this from personal experience. One comment I hear over and over from my own board members is "I like the way this board works. Assignments are interesting and well organized. I feel useful here."

I'm sure you have questions. Why don't I answer them now?

What you're saying about board members' involvement could apply to any nonprofit board operating under the Corporate Model, couldn't it?

Certainly. Only the details would change. For example, you can investigate the pros and cons of starting a new pilot program at Yorkville or you can investigate expanding program offerings at a nonprofit trade association.

Under the Model, the CEO and staff make all the operational decisions. Only rarely will board members be invited by the CEO to participate. Yet, doesn't the board still need to know what's going on in operations?

No doubt about it. The name of the game for the CEO is to communicate the important information to board members and to keep them informed of significant developments. Still, there's no need to clutter regular board meetings by reporting endless details about operations. Probably the most effective way of keeping board members aware of what is going on within the organization is to have staff frequently make short presentations at board meetings.

It's apparent to me that communication is a key issue here. Would you say the Model's structure contributes to a better flow of information?

Yes, it does. The Corporate Model structure has a built-in communication channel. You don't have just a few people at the top who really know what's going on in a dozen or two dozen different committees. Instead, you have two major committees—Assessment, Planning and Resource—channeling information to the third major committee—Executive—and then on to the full board. By the time an issue reaches the full board, it has been thoroughly reviewed by many different members. When directors know what's going on, they feel involved with the organization.

You've told us in your letters, and you've repeated it again today, that board meetings must be run in an efficient manner. How long do your regular monthly board meetings typically last?

I suspect you've all heard the old board proverb that "the number of board members who will attend the next regular meeting depends on how long the last one lasted." As CEO I always keep this proverb in mind. Our regular board meetings usually take one and one-quarter hours. Sometimes they run slightly longer.

Can you cite some examples showing when the CEO might invite board members to participate in operational decisions?

Let me give you one from my own experience. My non-profit organization, like so many others in this country, is faced with some severe funding cutbacks. My board decided it was time for our organization to hire a development specialist. Hiring such a person was obviously my responsibility.

However, I had no experience in hiring development specialists. Consequently, I invited two board members who do have such experience to advise me in this area. I was still responsible for the person I hired. If the new "hire" was a poor one, I couldn't blame the two board directors.

Everyone needs help to do his or her job from time to time. A CEO has to be mature enough to know his or her own limitations.

Jack, how about some other examples, more routine in nature, showing how directors can be invited to participate in operational areas?

Grant writing. Helping with media relations. Planning annual dinners.

I might use the term "displaced director" to refer to the board member who can't adapt to the Corporate Model and really wants to be involved with operations. Obviously, some displaced directors resign when the Model is adopted. But some don't. What do you do with them?

You involve them in ways that are perceived as being "hands on." For example, every CEO I know needs help telling the organization's story. If the board member is comfortable doing it, he or she can speak before groups.

Another way for him or her to participate is to be one of the directors responsible for the annual assessment of the nonprofit's financial situation.

Or suppose your board is investigating a major new service. Here's an opportunity to put your displaced director on the subcommittee investigating options. The director will be working closely with staff and dealing with an issue that directly impacts the people the organization serves.

If I recall correctly, in one of your letters you said the Corporate Model board should ideally include about 18 to 24 persons. Are all the members of your board truly involved?

I have 24 directors on my board. Not everyone is on a standing committee. Some directors are "held in reserve" to tackle special committee projects. These individuals are asked to get involved with one major project each year. The Executive Committee tries to appoint all new directors to a standing committee. This appointment gives them a thorough understanding of how our committee system works.

I'd say when a person first comes on our board he or she may feel uninvolved, but that doesn't last long. Right now, in fact, it seems as if everyone on my board is working on a specific task. It's been a particularly busy year for us.

On the other hand, I don't want to minimize the challenge for both the board chair and the CEO in keeping board directors involved. As I mentioned in my earlier correspondence with Russ, developing policy isn't inherently as interesting to many people as being involved in the operations of the organization. Consequently, the whole issue of involvement must be a priority issue for both the board chair and the CEO.

Russ has just given me a signal that our tee-off time is coming up soon. He's trying to tell me I'd better talk faster if I want to get in nine holes of golf before my plane leaves.

Actually, I think we've covered things pretty well this morning. Let me conclude by saying the adoption of the Corporate Model requires the chairperson and the president/CEO to give ongoing attention to maintaining the motivation of board members.

Board directors need to know their efforts translate into quality service for clients. Why? Because the board members most likely to feel a commitment are those who take pride in the organization and what it is doing.

Thanks for listening to me last night and again this morning. I hope that these sessions have been helpful.

6/14

Dear Jack,

Just want you to know the six of us on the restructuring committee have voted unanimously to recommend that the Yorkville board adopt the Corporate Model.

We are comfortable making that recommendation. More important, we're enthusiastic about it.

We are very hopeful that the Yorkville board will agree with our recommendation. At the very least, board discussions about the Model will force us to examine what our nonprofit board does and how it does it.

It may take some time before the full board makes a decision. When this happens, you will be one of the first to know.

Russ

P.S. I can't tell you how much I've appreciated your detailed responses to all of our questions. In particular, thanks for making a personal visit here. We all gained some very valuable insights. You state your case very persuasively!

6/18

Dear Russ,

I'm pleased about your recommendation! Keep me posted.

Jack

P.S. I'm particularly glad to have a copy of the transcript "Board Members Must Be Involved." When I discuss the Corporate Model, I get more questions about this area than any other. There's a good reason for that.

SO MANY DIRECTORS ON NONPROFIT BOARDS ARE BUSY PEO-PLE WITH DEMANDING SCHEDULES. THEY NEED TO HAVE CLEAR EVIDENCE THAT THEIR INVOLVEMENT IS MEANINGFUL AND MAKES A REAL DIFFERENCE FOR THE ORGANIZATION AND THE PEOPLE IT SERVES.

10/15

Dear Jack,

Finally, after exhaustive discussion, the Yorkville board has voted to adopt the Corporate Model!

The final vote was last night. The members of the restructuring group were elated. The final tally was 25 directors in favor of the Model, five opposed.

We've got a long road ahead of us, but at least we're *finally* on the right path.

We couldn't have done it without you!

Russ

P.S. Will fill you in on more details when I see you at parents' weekend later this month. My son seems to be adjusting to college life!

9

THE CORPORATE MODEL

Two Years Later

9/30 (two years later)

Dear Jack,

It's hard to believe it's been nearly two years since we adopted the Model!

I'm happy to respond to your recent note asking for written comments about Yorkville's experiences with its new governance structure.

And by the way, before I give you my update, I want to congratulate you on being invited to speak about the Corporate Model at your annual meeting. A national address before 1,000 people is pretty impressive. What's more, I think they definitely asked the right person to speak!

I like your idea of surveying other organizations that adopted the Model and summarizing their personal experiences as part of your speech. I'd love to know what you find out, so I can share it with my fellow board members and our CEO. I'm sure the members of the restructuring committee who helped investigate the Model for Yorkville would be especially interested.

So here's my contribution to your speech.

YORKVILLE: THE MODEL PLUS TWO YEARS

You were right. Change was a challenge. Many of the things you said would happen did, in fact, occur. Among other things, our board chairperson was hard to win over to the new way of doing things. He completed his term, but asked not to be considered for re-election to the board.

We also lost two long-time board members. One resigned, saying he wished things at Yorkville "could be the way they used to be, when we really felt we were part owners of the place." The other director was "not particularly interested in setting policy." Yet, I'm very happy to report, Yorkville is a much, much stronger organization today than it was when I joined the board.

- Our fiscal problems are under control.
- We've strengthened many programs and eliminated several outmoded ones.
- The board is achieving more, in less time.
- Assessment is much more rigorous.

We no longer have the hastily prepared questionnaire or the check-off type of evaluation that used to be typical for our organization.

We've been particularly fortunate to have Joyce Thomas. She has grown professionally in the position and is an excellent president and CEO.

We're also fortunate to have a new board chairperson who is committed to making the Model work. The following story, which happened recently, should give you a good sense of his commitment.

A new board member made an end run to a staff member, saying he really wanted to be involved in programming. The staff member asked the director "to talk to the head of the board."

Within 24 hours, the board chair called me and asked if I would share a copy of our correspondence, the very letters that led Yorkville to adopt the Corporate Model. The board chair said, "Jim's new and so used to doing things the traditional way, I want to give him a full understanding of a volunteer director's role under the Model." I was more than happy to oblige.

In the relatively brief time we've had the Model, I've really come to appreciate the continuing importance of communication at every level in the organization. I know you made it clear to us two years ago that communication really is a key ingredient in the culture change.

To give you an example of another type of communication, I've attached a copy of a letter the new board chair recently sent to the Yorkville staff.

Russ

September 6

Dear _____,

This summer, the Assessment Committee recommended that our organization communicate more with staff about the vastly different roles of the board and management at Yorkville. The recommendation grew out of discussions held with management following the recent staff survey.

President Joyce Thomas will soon inaugurate a new communication program. This letter will give you an overview of the Corporate Model, the unusual and innovative board/management structure adopted by Yorkville two years ago.

Under this structure, the board formulates policy and evaluates the organization's operations in carrying out policy. This means that all proposed programs are reviewed by the board's Planning and Resource Committee as to their feasibility. If approved at this level, new programs are sent to the Executive Committee, and then to the full board for discussion and final approval.

New policies under which the organization must operate are usually developed by ad hoc committees. They are reviewed by the Planning and Resource Committee. The Executive Committee provides the next level of review, after which the policies are sent to the full board with comments for final approval. If policies are approved by the full board, it becomes management's responsibility to see that they are executed properly.

Joyce Thomas is president/chief executive officer and a voting member of the board. She has complete authority over, and responsibility for, all management decisions and functions.

She directs the operations of our nonprofit organization in accordance with policy established by the board.

Our structure provides for the annual review of policies and for evaluating achievements against goals.

The board's Assessment Committee is charged with reviewing policies to verify that they are being carried out by management and staff as originally intended. The same committee is also responsible for recommending whether Yorkville should continue, revamp, or discontinue existing programs.

The past two years have been extremely busy for Yorkville. We have clarified responsibilities, started new programs, and discontinued others. We've achieved some major goals and fiscal savings. We have been able to avoid staff layoffs.

The board recognizes that its new board/management relationship has led to many changes. Change inevitably created some stress within the organization. The Yorkville board of directors is very much aware of the difficult job the staff has had in these many months of change. We value the spirit of cooperation among staff throughout this period.

Yorkville is moving ahead. In very large measure, our successes are the direct result of the cooperation and dedication you show in meeting your own responsibilities.

Sincerely,

Chairperson
Yorkville Board of Directors

10/12

Dear Russ,

Thanks for your quick response to my request for a written update on your experience with the Model. I'll get back to you with comments.

Your chairperson's letter makes it clear that Yorkville knows where it is today—and where it's going in the future.

I congratulate your board on all that it has achieved.

Jack

P.S.   YOUR ORGANIZATION IS NOW IN WORKING ORDER. YOU HAVE SEPARATED POLICY FROM PAPER CLIPS, AND YOU ARE READY FOR THE NEW CENTURY!

10

THE MODEL IN ACTION

Real Life Experiences

11/15

Dear Russ,

I gave my speech a few days ago, and though I'm biased, I'd say it went over well. I've had a lot of positive feedback. People were especially interested in the comments of individuals who really live with this Model.

Because I drew heavily on our correspondence of two years ago in the early part of the speech, I spoke from notes about how the Model is constructed. I ended the first half of the speech by reading parts of your recent letter, with the names deleted.

Enclosed is an excerpt from the second half of the speech. It's based on actual comments of nonprofit presidents/CEOs who use the Model. My goal in this part of the speech was to give the audience some feel for how other president/CEOs view the Model in practice. It's the only part of the speech I drafted completely.

Feel free to share these comments on real life experiences with your colleagues on the board and with Yorkville management.

Jack

THE CORPORATE MODEL IN PRACTICE

Whenever I talk about the Corporate Model, I always look for the people in the crowd who are shaking their head as if to say, "It works for him, but how do we know it works for other people and groups?"

Every large crowd has skeptics, and I can see this audience is no exception. But I did some extra homework and came prepared to answer your questions.

Up to this point I've talked primarily about the role of the board under the Model, using a number of telling comments from my friend Russ. So now it's management's turn at the podium.

William Bowen, the president of the Andrew W. Mellon Foundation and former Princeton University president, recently said that "finding the appropriate balance between executive authority and board oversight is more likely to require strengthening the hand of the CEO than building up the powers of the board."

When I was asked to speak, I knew I wanted to describe in a very tangible way what the impact of strengthening the CEO's hand means to an organization. At the same time, I wanted you to get the sense that the Model does not come in only plain vanilla; it comes in a rainbow of flavors.

So about six weeks ago I sat down and made a list of not-for-profit groups operating under the Model. I pared my list to 11 groups that vary in terms of size, budget, and the length of time they've operated under the Model.

Most of them have about 100 employees, although they range from a low of 70 staff members to a high of 2,000 employees. Their annual budgets range from $1.5 million to $50 million, with a number of organizations clustered around the $4.5 million mark. Their time with the Model is as brief as two years and as long as 10 years.

After making my list, I called the 11 president/CEOs heading these organizations. I asked about 10 questions, from "How Well Has the Model Served Your Organization?" to "What Are the Financial Benefits?" But these questions were just to frame the interview. What I was really looking for was their take on their own experience.

Every one of them reported they are happy with the Model, but two said they would be happier if their nonprofits had made them voting members of the board. One commented, however, that not being a board member made it possible for her to advocate for her organization's mission and not be constrained by fiscal concerns.

Although this may seem like an unusual viewpoint, this CEO finds some value in acting essentially as an outside consultant would act. I know from her later comments that on a day-to-day basis, she is not actually free from fiscal constraints. Like the others I interviewed, she's counting dollars carefully these days.

Every organization I interviewed had reduced its committee structure. One had gone so far as to have only two standing committees, while another had cut back to EIGHT. Virtually everyone, it seemed, was happiest about getting rid of their personnel committees.

What impressed me most, however, was how consistently they felt the board structure had empowered them and their organizations. Here are some of their comments . . .

"It assisted us in the rapid development of a work plan. The Model appeals to 'fast track' board people who want to get things done."

"It has freed me to take our mission and policies and implement them in an efficient way."

"With the Model, we have the ability to be more competitive in a rapidly changing environment."

"As president, I have clout when dealing with others. The title gives me entree to and equity with business executives."

And finally, a very poignant comment from a CEO who finds that the Corporate Model provides a very different work environment from what he'd known in the traditional nonprofit world.

"The Model," he said, *"gets away from the 'Do what we want you to do' syndrome."*

Another impression gained from these interviews was how clearly everyone understood their roles. Over and over, execs mentioned that the line between staff and board members was no longer fuzzy. The Model had clearly defined CEO, board director, and staff roles. In the words of one exec, the Model "defines the roles of the players extremely well and determines what is appropriate or not."

Staff members, one manager noted, also feel like empowered professionals. The overall message was that management in these organizations is spending more time doing things that need to be done rather than spending a daunting amount of time responding to board requests.

While doing these interviews—they took about 30 to 45 minutes for each one—I refrained from making comments of my own about the Model. I wanted their words, not mine.

When I asked, "What are the differences between the Corporate Model and the traditional or community model? These are the responses I received:

"It's more efficient. There's so much to be done. It conserves time resources. The community model encumbered management. This makes wise use of volunteer time."

"I wouldn't work under the community model. The emotional connection often fostered under the community model is not necessarily good."

"People in the business world really understand how it works. That's a built-in advantage."

"It requires the president to be more of a risk-taker."

"There's more emphasis on strategy."

All of this sounds pretty good. But obviously, any governance structure that is this different has disadvantages as well as advantages. Or if you're an optimist, as I am, you'll consider them problems to overcome.

Maintaining connection with board members is simply easier to do, one respondent said, with the "feel good" approach of the community model. There's also an adjustment period for board members who have "extra" time on their hands and who want to be operationally involved, some noted.

A colleague of mine once observed that directors who have too much time to contribute can be just as much a problem as directors who don't have enough time. I'm sure many of you can relate to either of these scenarios.

The other two major disadvantages I heard about in my interviews can be summarized in these two statements:

"Fund raising can be more difficult because there's less involvement."

"The Corporate Model is too cognitive in character . . . the heart is missing."

At the same time, the executives often countered these statements, with action-oriented language of their own.

Statements like "When it comes to fund raising, the president just needs to motivate board members to do the job." Or this statement, which actually parallels my own view . . .

"Finding responsible and useful tasks for people who take board positions to 'feel good' about what they are doing will always be a challenge."

Many of the people I interviewed were pleased with the way the Corporate Model has helped their organizations grow. Several noted their not-for-profit groups had tripled or quadrupled in size over the course of a few years. These same execs said their organizations were not growing under the community model. But growth within the organization actually was defined in different ways by different execs.

"Our organization is clearly more entrepreneurial. This opens doors in the business world. Business titles . . . enable you to approach business people or donors without feeling you're going 'hat-in-hand.'"

Others pointed out the Model helped them attract very talented people to the nonprofit sector. Many of these same recruits, they told me, were turned off by the traditional model and its slow decision-making processes.

And finally, one said his organization just gets more respect. "The United Way and others respect a policy-making board when they review one."

I also asked my interviewees if they could list some financial benefits of the Corporate Model. They noted the routine savings, like not having to buy as many lunches for board members or not spending "$1,000 in process costs to save $100."

They also spoke of more dramatic financial benefits. One not-for-profit exec said that his nonprofit had been dependent on the United Way for 70 percent of its funds before adopting the Corporate Model, but now needed only 30 percent of its funds from this charitable organization.

Another CEO said her nonprofit is now well positioned to sell services to business organizations. Others reported savings related to staff administrative time, which they estimated at about three to four days per month.

My final questions were about the effectiveness of the assessment process and the time it took their organizations to move to the Corporate Model. In both cases, the responses varied significantly.

One group said its board does not have either an assessment process or an assessment committee. It depends on the United Way as well as state and national accrediting processes to evaluate the organization. Others have very rigorous processes to evaluate both internal and external environments. Many look to progress in their strategic plans to set the benchmarks for evaluations.

Overall, these 11 nonprofits moved to the Corporate Model in as short a period as one year or as long as five years.

The way it happened in all cases can be summed up in a single phrase: STRONG LEADERSHIP MADE IT HAPPEN!

11

THE MODEL VS. TRADITION

An Overview

Of the Differences

11/20

Dear Russ,

When I sent the excerpt from my speech highlighting the comments of president/CEOs in the real world, I forgot to include something I think you'll find interesting.

I put together a special handout for distribution at the national meeting. It simply lists the important differences—nearly 40 of them—between the Corporate Model and the traditional nonprofit model.

Thought you'd enjoy seeing it.

Jack

CORPORATE MODEL VS. TRADITIONAL MODEL
WHAT'S DIFFERENT?

Board Involvement and Communication

CORPORATE	TRADITIONAL
Represents New Approach to Board Governance	*Has Strength through Years of Tradition*
Simplifies Board Organization Structure	*Creates Complex Board Organization Structure*
Utilizes Board Talents for Policy Issues	*Has Board Addressing Policy & Operations*
Does Not Involve Board in Operations	*Takes Staff Time to Orient, Educate Board*
Makes Use of Staff Input for Key Decisions	*Places Lower Value on Staff Input*
Allows for Fewer Board Members	*Allows for Greater Number of Board Members*
Keeps Communication Line Clear	*Tends to Create Complex Lines of Communication*
Includes Fewer Topics on Board Agendas	*Often Includes Minor Operating Items on Agenda*
Reduces Time Needed to Make Decisions	*Have to Increase Time to Make Decisions*
Board: Hires Only CEO	*Hires CEO, Other Personnel*
Board Assesses CEO and Organization Rigorously	*Board Assesses Management More Informally*

Management of the Organization

CORPORATE

Formally Structures Organization

Pinpoints Responsibility and Clarifies Accountability

Builds Staff Professionalism

Allows for More Management Flexibility

Allows Top Executive to Be More of a Risk Taker

Makes Full-Time Manager President/CEO

Orients CEO to Strong Management Style

More Ad Hoc Committees, But Fewer Standing Committees

Reduces Staff Time Spent Supporting Committees

Increases Focus on Productivity

Provides a Board Structure For Growth

TRADITIONAL

Develops Less Formal Organization

Promotes Shared Responsibility and Shared Blame

Board Can Direct Staff— Can Be "Servants"

Managers Must Often Wait for Board to Act

Board & Exec Share Risk-Taking Responsibility

Makes Volunteer Director President/CEO

Board Involvement Allows for Weaker Top Executive

Leads to Many Standing Committees

Staff Spends Much Time Supporting Committees

Puts More Focus on "Feelings"

During Growth Periods, Tends to Create Operating Difficulties

Financial Operations

CORPORATE	**TRADITIONAL**
Creates Bottom-Up Budget Process	*Establishes Top-Down Budget Process*
Establishes System of Checks and Balances	*Allows for Informal Checks and Balances*
Except for Budget, Does Not Involve Board in Fiscal Processes	*Involves Board in Many Fiscal Processes, e.g. Signing Checks*
Is Cost Effective	*Is Not Cost Effective*

Interpersonal Relationships

CORPORATE	**TRADITIONAL**
Trust Is a Critical Factor in Culture	*Board & Exec Have Parent–Child Relationship*
Full-Time Manager Is Board Member, Often with Voting Status	*Does Not Include Full-Time Manager As a Member of the Board*
Takes More Effort to Develop Relationships between Directors and Members of Organization	*Makes Establishing Interpersonal Relationships Easier Because of Involvement*
CEO Serves as Full-Time Spokesperson	*Volunteer President Is Part-Time Spokesperson*
Corporate Titles Speak Clearly to Public	*Titles (Administrator, Executive Secretary) Aren't Clear to Public*

Interpersonal Relationships, cont.

CORPORATE

CEO Can Overstep Boundaries

Says "End-Runs" of Staff to Board Are Unacceptable Practices

Challenges CEO to Maintain Commitment of Individual Board Directors

TRADITIONAL

Top Manager's Role Is Well-Defined

"End-Runs" of Staff to Board Are Accepted Practices

Reduces the Challenge in Keeping Individual Board Members Committed to the Organization

Policy Development

CORPORATE

Sets Framework for Clear Separation of Policy and Operations

Gives Planning Issues Priority

Puts Major Focus on Clients/Members

TRADITIONAL

Tradition Defines Management Patterns and Rules

Allows Planning Discussions to Be Postponed

Puts Major Focus on Process

12

IS YOUR ORGANIZATION READY
FOR THE CORPORATE MODEL?

The following questions and answers can further help
you assess whether the Corporate Model is right for your
organization. In attempting to apply this information,
you should take into account the personalities, the culture, and the management situation in your own organization. The Corporate Model is not only about structure;
it is also about people, which is why no book about the
Corporate Model can ever be truly complete. Each nonprofit organization that adopts the Model must write its
own ending.

*Q. I thought there was only one Corporate Model. Can it be
utilized in different ways?*
A. The Corporate Model has one general framework. Its
major feature is the separation of policy and operations.
How this separation is accomplished can vary from organization to organization. In addition, four other charac-
teristics clearly distinguish the Corporate Model from
more traditional board structures. These are: fewer committees, fewer board meetings, fewer "surprises," and
greater top-management accountability.

*Q. What kinds of nonprofit boards are most likely to be attract-
ed to the Corporate Model?*
A. Nonprofit boards experiencing some internal dissen-
sion and boards that are constantly bogged down in
detail. Also, the Corporate Model will appeal to many
nonprofit boards that are operating satisfactorily, but
wish to become more efficient and effective. Members of

these boards realize that with the Corporate Model, they could be even more productive.

Q. Nonprofit X has a board in name only. Board members are prominent individuals, but not very active. The organization now finds it needs more involvement from its board. Will the Corporate Model work for this organization?

A. Yes. Discuss the Corporate Model with all board members. Talk about the various responsibilities directors have and, in particular, the board's policy-making function. Explain that the Model enables the president/CEO to request board members' time only for the development and assessment of policy issues. The key points to stress are that their time commitments will not be extensive and wise use will be made of the time they do give to the organization.

Q. Very often the people who serve on for-profit boards are the same people who serve on nonprofit boards. Given this scenario, why have so many volunteer directors tended, over time, to function less efficiently on nonprofit boards than on for-profit boards?

A. It has a great deal to do with tradition and the level of financial risk involved. In for-profit groups, directors may well have a personal, financial stake in the success of the organization. They can be financially at risk if the organization is operated inefficiently or ineffectively. Generally, unless they make very negligent decisions, nonprofit boards are not at risk financially.

Q. How long does it take to institute the Corporate Model?
A. It generally takes about a year from the time the board adopts it. Change never occurs steadily or smoothly. There are always highs and lows in the process. Remember, it takes education and constant repetition to make the Model more than a structural outline. It also takes leadership and persuasion to make the Model work. The role of the board chairperson in this process is critical. Also remember that the Model needs to be reassessed about every five years. If new board members do not fully understand the Model, the board may tend to fall back into traditional ways of operating.

Q. How long does it take to be completely comfortable with the Corporate Model?
A. It takes at least several years of operation. It may take some boards even longer—to the point where all directors have come on the board under the Corporate Model structure.

Q. What types of board members are most likely to oppose the adoption of the Corporate Model?
A. Some "process" people, those who are never quite done examining things from all angles, tend to hold back their full approval for the Corporate Model. Though they don't view it this way, they tend to like the hands-on involvement that comes from the parent–child board structure.

Some directors may be hostile to the concept because they do not want to give up power. Some of these individuals may not exercise managerial direction in their own jobs. Others are not satisfied with their jobs and seek satisfaction through their work on a nonprofit board. They may not want to give up the influence they can exercise over operations in the nonprofit organization.

Q. What do you do about a truly hostile board member—one staunchly opposed to the Model even though it has been adopted?
A. Whatever the reason for the hostility, it is difficult to have such a personality on your board. Sometimes these individuals can be convinced by other directors whom they respect that the organization is better served by the Model. Sometimes diplomacy, particularly on the part of the board chairperson, is sufficient. Other times you can only wait until their terms expire or they decide to leave the board.

Q. What types of board members do you want on the Corporate Model board?
A. No particular personality or occupational type suits the Corporate Model. Board directors who have operated well under the Model include full-time homemakers, ministers, labor leaders, human service personnel, physicians, community volunteers, and others. The common denominator that makes individuals effective as board directors is their interest in establishing and monitoring policy.

Conversely, these same individuals often have a low tolerance for being involved with operational details, i.e., the paper clips and computer disks of the operation.

Usually they understand the importance of addressing issues in terms of concept and/or strategy.

Most important, these individuals can work within a policy environment without becoming bored. They like having a good handle on the organization's direction. They have little need for the continual interpersonal operational interaction and immediate operational gratification that characterize the culture of the traditional nonprofit board. The truly outstanding Corporate Model board directors have excellent vision.

While a broad range of talents and skills are needed on the traditional board to address operational needs, it is not quite the same for boards operating under the Model. Although you want diversity, in terms of individual backgrounds and development skills and contacts, you need to keep one requirement in focus when recruiting new directors. You need individuals with vision.

Q. What does the meeting agenda typically include for a board operating under the Corporate Model?
A. When setting the agenda, remember that you have two chief objectives: to stay focused on policy issues and to conserve board members' time. Use the following outline when you determine the flow of your board meetings.

Meeting Flow
- Review of last meeting minutes
- Review of financial statements
- Old Business

- New Business
    Report by President on Operations
    Reports by other managers
    (e.g., medical director)
- Board training

Q. How often should a Corporate Model board meet?
A. In general, Corporate Model boards meet less often than do boards structured under the traditional model. Not-for-profit groups operating in a local area tend to find six to eight meetings a year sufficient. Some organizations have gone to quarterly meetings, but very often this level of contact is insufficient to build a cohesive team spirit among volunteer directors. Some national groups meet only two times a year. However, many national groups have found they need to hold board meetings more often than every six months.

Regardless of how many meetings a board has, the Model requires more meetings for ad hoc committees and the Executive Committee. These are key meetings, during which the most basic work takes place.

Because of time-compressed lifestyles and travel expenses, some regional and national nonprofit organizations have begun to hold meetings via conference call or electronic media. How these changes will impact an organization's productivity and effectiveness remains to be seen.

Q. Do Corporate Model boards set a dollar limit on the president/CEO's fiscal discretion?

A. The president/CEO has complete discretion as long as he or she works within the budget and budgetary guidelines. However, if any major changes are needed, the board must approve them. For example, if the president/CEO finds resources budgeted for capital improvements are not needed, he or she cannot simply move these funds to the salary account without board approval.

Most organizations need to borrow money on a short-term basis to meet cash-flow requirements. The CEO needs to have complete discretion to act in such situations. Consequently, the board needs to pass a formal resolution authorizing a fiscal limit for borrowing. In practice, this limit is typically dependent upon the needs of the organization and the level of confidence the board has in the CEO!

Q. What happens when a nonprofit organization changes presidents?
A. The board must find a new president who understands the Corporate Model and feels secure with it. This individual must be a strong person. Immediately, he or she will be faced with a whole set of responsibilities not generally found in a more traditional structure. The person must want and be able to assume this level of responsibility.

Q. How is the president/CEO's job description developed?
A. By the Executive Committee or an ad hoc committee, with final approval by the full board. It must reflect the

needs of the nonprofit organization and should be reviewed periodically by the board. The CEO can also request a change. Such requests are usually related to growth in the organization.

Q. Is the Corporate Model situational? Would it work fine for President A, but have to be modified considerably for President B?
A. No. The Corporate Model is adopted for the organization, not the individual. When a not-for-profit organization chooses a new president, it requires that the responsibilities of the new president/CEO be the same as those of the old one. A crucial requirement for the Corporate Model board is to find the right person to do the job.

Q. Under the Corporate Model, how should the board respond if the president/CEO makes a mistake?
A. No one does a job perfectly. If this mistake is one in a series of serious errors, the president/CEO might need to be replaced. Directors should consider the CEO's total record and carefully weigh the seriousness of the mistake.

Q. How does a president/CEO turn down advice about operations from the board?
A. With difficulty. It all depends on the kind of culture that has been established on the board. Ideally, the president/CEO should be comfortable saying, "Thank you for your suggestions. I have considered them, but I feel these matters should be handled differently." A culture of mutual trust has to be nurtured so that the president

and the board accept the separation of operations from policy. The board chairperson plays a key role in developing this culture.

Q. *Does the Corporate Model board ever take over for an inept president?*
A. The board may have to become involved if it dismisses a president. The arrangement is temporary and continues only until a replacement can be hired. Otherwise, the board has no excuse for becoming involved in management. If the board has to manage for the president, then that president shouldn't be there.

Q. *How does the Corporate Model board know when to discharge a president/CEO?*
A. When the president is not meeting agreed goals and objectives or is meeting them in an illegal, immoral, or inept way. Leadership is critical. You'll know if it's missing.

Q. *Can a board member ever wear another "hat" in an organization?*
A. Sometimes a board member acts not as a director but as a different kind of volunteer. For example, Director Z has a particular accounting skill and wants to utilize it to help the nonprofit. The CEO agrees. In this instance, the board member is not a board member, but a volunteer working under the direction of the CEO.

This distinction is easy to understand if you think about the example of a Boy Scout leader who serves as a troop's scoutmaster and also serves as a board member on a Boy Scout regional council. As scoutmaster he follows scouting guidelines and directives from the professionals. As a council director he helps set policy for the Scout movement in that geographic area. In both instances, he is a volunteer. In only one instance does he act as a director.

Q. When can board members get involved in operational areas?
A. Only when they are invited to do so by the president/CEO. At these times, let me stress again, they are not acting as board members.

Q. How are reasonable disagreements over whether an issue is a policy or operational question resolved?
A. The board makes the final decision on where to draw the line. In a case of opposing views, it's up to the CEO to make the most persuasive argument for his or her position. Though the board and president/CEO are partners, the board is the ultimate authority.

Q. How do you persuade an unusually influential board member to reduce his or her interest in operational issues?
A. Every board has this problem. The Corporate Model board is no exception. Every situation is handled according to the personality involved. Proceed with great care.

Q. How is board succession handled under the Model?
A. In very much the same manner as under the traditional model. Typically, directors serve either two or

three three-year terms. In some nonprofits, directors can be re-elected after a full year's absence from the board. This procedure is not recommended for the Corporate Model board because the Model depends on a flow of new ideas and viewpoints.

Boards need to be aware of the need to keep the Model's structure intact. As new directors with traditional board experience come aboard, there may be a tendency to add more board standing committees. Adding more and more committees will eventually undermine the structure—and defeat the purpose of the Model. As a result, the structure can return to a traditional one without anyone ever casting a vote for the change.

Because the CEO is likely to be the person who is the one "constant" throughout turnover of volunteers and staff, he or she is responsible for working with the board chair to train and educate new directors in the processes and values of the Corporate Model. This ongoing educational process must continue for years because the Model is still considered a new and, to some people, radical structure of governance.

Q. What if the staff complains that the organization has become "too formal" under the Corporate Model?
A. The Model is a formal structure but it is also a human one. Any organization that grows and becomes more complex needs a more formal structure and a clearly defined communication channel. The Model provides both. Communication is critically important. The CEO,

in particular, must be very aware of the need to communicate effectively with all parts of the organization. The Corporate Model sounds businesslike, but it is not cold and uncaring.

Q. Doesn't the Corporate Model mimic what takes place in the profit sector?
A. To some extent, yes, but with one key difference. The Corporate Model board in the nonprofit arena must conduct a finer performance audit than most business organizations conduct. That's because there is no fiscal bottom line on which to judge performance. In addition, so much of what a nonprofit does must ultimately be measured with qualitative information or with rough quantitative data.

Q. If a traditionally structured not-for-profit group isn't ready to adopt the full Corporate Model, can it compromise and adopt parts of the Model?
A. Boards in this situation can take three steps and still benefit significantly.

First, within the current structure, try to give more responsibilities to the executive director. Examine all powers and responsibilities now held by the board and determine where shifts can be made. Ask questions: Does the board really need a physical facilities committee? Can responsibility for physical facilities be delegated to management with intermittent oversight by the board?

The next step is to review the board's entire committee structure. Are all the committees the board currently has necessary? How many committees are wasting valuable volunteer time? All too frequently, committees are established simply because managers want "to keep volunteers involved." If you examine the activities of these committees, you'll find they generally amount to nothing more than "busy work." Make sure every board committee, over time, is making wise use of volunteer time.

The third and most important step is to ensure that the board rigorously evaluates the CEO and the organization. The volunteer president (or board chair) should not be doing it alone. Evaluation should be done by a committee that assesses and analyzes every important aspect of the organization in some depth. The overall objective of the committee should be to assess policy outcomes—not count paper clips.

Q. Why is the Corporate Model sometimes called the "Model of Accountability"?
A. On more traditional boards, whose directors participate in operational decisions, it is difficult to determine responsibility. The Corporate Model pinpoints accountability much better than any other nonprofit board structure. When it is properly utilized, there is little equivocation as to who is responsible.

Q. Across the U.S., nonprofits have been slow to adopt the Corporate Model. Why?
A. There are many reasons, including tradition, executive director reluctance, rhetoric, and human inertia.

When it comes to making a cultural change, tradition is a powerful master. Individuals who have been involved with the traditional model understand it and are comfortable with the way it operates. Despite its many limitations, it is still a known quantity. In addition, involvement with the details of the organization's activities is often very interesting and appealing to many volunteers. That makes it easy for volunteer directors to overlook the fact that the board structure is less results oriented than it could be.

Another reason for the slow growth of the Corporate Model is the reluctance of executive directors to assume more responsibility. It is not unusual for an executive director in a traditionally structured nonprofit to be shocked at the level of responsibility the executive head of the Corporate Model organization must shoulder. Many executive directors are comfortable presenting alternatives to the board, then withdrawing from the decision-making process. This is a "safe" way to operate. If the board makes a poor decision, the executive director can't be blamed. On the other hand, if the decision is on target, it's easy for the executive director to claim credit because he or she recommended it in the first place.

Rhetoric is another factor. This simply means that when the benefits of the Corporate Model are discussed, too many people talk it to death by calling for "volunteer involvement" and "organization ownership."

The final factor is human inertia—probably the biggest barrier for the Corporate Model. Change is difficult and stressful; many directors simply don't want to address the need for change on their boards.

Q. What is the single most important advantage of the Corporate Model?
A. It makes your nonprofit look ahead to the future.

Since our switch to the Model we've served more people at less time and cost.

ABOUT THE AUTHORS

Eugene H. Fram, Ed.D., J. Warren McClure Research Professor of Marketing at Rochester (N.Y.) Institute of Technology, is an authority on the Corporate Model. His experience with nonprofit organizations—as consultant, board director, and board chair—dates back more than 20 years. In addition, he has extensive experience working with business boards of directors. He pioneered the development of the Corporate Model for nonprofit organizations. A frequent lecturer on the Model, Dr. Fram has published articles on the topic for professional journals.

Vicki Brown has been writing professionally for 25 years. She has been a newspaper reporter, free-lance writer, editor, and public relations specialist. She now operates her own firm, *Word Impressions,* in Rochester, New York. She has long had a special interest in working with nonprofit groups. In addition, she writes for a variety of business, medical, and educational organizations.